GEORGE WHITEFIELD

Pioneering Evangelist

Bruce and Becky Durost Fish

BARBOUR
PUBLISHING, INC.
Uhrichsville, Ohio

Other books in the "Heroes of the Faith" series:

Brother Andrew	*Martin Luther*
Gladys Aylward	*D. L. Moody*
William and Catherine Booth	*Samuel Morris*
John Bunyan	*George Müller*
William Carey	*Watchman Nee*
Amy Carmichael	*John Newton*
George Washington Carver	*Florence Nightingale*
Fanny Crosby	*Mary Slessor*
Frederick Douglass	*Charles Spurgeon*
Jonathan Edwards	*Hudson Taylor*
Jim Elliot	*William Tyndale*
Charles Finney	*Corrie ten Boom*
Billy Graham	*Mother Teresa*
C. S. Lewis	*Sojourner Truth*
Eric Liddell	*John Wesley*
David Livingstone	

©2000 by Barbour Publishing, Inc.

ISBN 1-57748-735-4

Published by Barbour Publishing, Inc., P.O. Box 719, Uhrichsville, OH 44683
http://www.barbourbooks.com

Cover illustration © Dick Bobnick.

ecpa Member of the
Evangelical Christian
Publishers Association

Printed in the United States of America.

GEORGE
WHITEFIELD

introduction

Silence gripped the six thousand people standing outside during a cold fall evening in November 1739. They filled the Philadelphia streets surrounding the courthouse steps. Lamps provided minimal light, and every eye strained toward the top of the stairs. A small figure stood calmly, his words riveting the crowd's attention.

Those fortunate enough to be close by saw a young man nearing his twenty-fifth birthday, dressed in dark clerical robes and wearing a powdered wig. He was fine-boned and slight, with a hawkish nose. His left eye tended to turn inward, the permanent legacy of a bad case of childhood measles.

But his voice overcame any physical imperfections. When George Whitefield spoke, people thought they heard music. His clear tones carried to the farthest person in the crowd. Sometimes he whispered intently. Other times his voice resounded with passion.

The vast majority of people in his American audiences had never seen a theatrical performance of any type. No permanent theaters existed in the colonies. There were no professional troupes of actors in America. Because they were not familiar with dramatic techniques of delivery, these people found George Whitefield's sermons to be a revelation. They hung on his every word.

Whitefield never used notes, a great departure from the well-established tradition of reading sermons. Often, he acted out the lives of biblical figures. Using gestures, tears, body movements, and changes of inflection in his voice, he transported his listeners to another time. They were with the person he described and faced the same struggles and temptations. While ministers of his day were taught to present careful, reasoned arguments in their sermons, Whitefield strove to engage his listeners' emotions. He yearned to make people understand the love of God and to create in them a desire for a personal relationship with Jesus Christ.

On this night he preached "Abraham Offering His Son," one of his favorite sermons for audiences in the American colonies. First, Whitefield described Abraham and Isaac walking to the mountain where Abraham intended to sacrifice his son. "The good old man [walked] with his dear child. . .now and then looking upon him, loving him, and then turning aside to weep." Whitefield paused, allowing his audience to feel the gravity of Abraham's situation.

He next described Abraham tying Isaac to the altar. Then came the moment when Abraham prepared to sacrifice his only son. "Fancy that you saw the aged parent standing by weeping. . . . Methinks I see the tears trickle down the patriarch Abraham's cheeks."

Never before had the people understood Abraham's pain so personally.

"Did you weep just now when I bid you fancy that you saw the altar?" George Whitefield asked. "Look up by faith, behold the blessed Jesus, our all-glorious Immanuel, not bound, but nailed on an accursed tree: See how he hangs crowned with thorns, and had in derision of all that are round about him: See how the thorns pierce him, and how the blood in purple streams trickles down his sacred temples! Hark! And now where are all your tears? Shall I refrain your voice from weeping? No, rather let me exhort you to look to him whom you have pierced, and mourn, as a woman mourneth for her first born."[1]

No one moved. Half the city of Philadelphia had turned out to hear this famous young preacher from England. Some were merely curious. Others wanted to hear for themselves the person whose name filled their local papers. Whatever their original motives for attending, suddenly they were confronted with the truth of the gospel in a way they had not expected. Christianity became a personal response to Jesus Christ, not simply a set of doctrinal beliefs.

One person who frequently listened to George White-field's preaching in Philadelphia that fall was a thirty-three-year-old printer named Benjamin Franklin. Tall, robust, and athletic, Ben Franklin differed in his appearance from Whitefield as much as he did in his view of God. Franklin was a deist who valued religious faith for the positive influence it had on society. He doubted that God could be known in a personal way.

Franklin also questioned everything. He had read reports of the huge crowds who had listened to Whitefield in the fields of England. Wondering if one person's voice could be clearly heard by so many people, Franklin decided to conduct an experiment. "[Whitefield] preached one evening from the top of the courthouse steps, which are in the middle of Market Street and on the west side of Second Street, which crosses it at right angles," Franklin reported. "Being among the hindmost in Market Street, I had the curiosity to learn how far he could be heard, by retiring backwards down the street towards the river; and I found his voice distinct till I came near Front Street, when some noise in that street obscured it. Imagining then a semicircle, of which my distance should be the radius, and that it were filled with auditors to each of whom I allowed two square feet, I computed that he might be heard by more than thirty thousand. This reconciled me to the newspaper accounts of his having preached to twenty-five thousand people in the fields, and to the ancient stories of generals haranguing whole armies, of which I had sometimes doubted."

Soon Franklin began printing George Whitefield's sermons and journals. This was the beginning of a friendship between the two men that lasted until Whitefield's death. Whenever Whitefield arrived in Philadelphia, he was a welcomed guest at Franklin's home. When churches closed their doors to Whitefield's ministry, Franklin helped build a hall where Whitefield and other itinerant speakers could address the citizens of Philadelphia.

The correspondence between the two men stretched out over decades. Whitefield often admonished Franklin to look to the health of his soul. Franklin, in turn, pleaded with Whitefield to look to the health of his body. Neither convinced the other to change his ways, but they respected and admired the improvements each brought to the lives of thousands of ordinary people.

"The multitudes of all sects and denominations that attended his sermons were enormous," Franklin observed after Whitefield's first visit to Philadelphia. "And it was matter of speculation to me, who was one of the number, to observe the extraordinary influence of his oratory on his hearers, and how much they admired and respected him, notwithstanding his common abuse of them by assuring them that they were naturally half beasts and half devils. It was wonderful to see the change soon made in the manners of our inhabitants. From being thoughtless or indifferent about religion, it seemed as if all the world were growing religious, so that one could not walk through the town in an evening without hearing psalms sung in different families of every street."

As Whitefield preached throughout the American colonies, thousands of individuals heeded his words. Whitefield's sermons built upon the foundation of a revival that began with the preaching of Jonathan Edwards and other colonial ministers. So many colonists turned to Christ during this period that the revival became known as the "Great Awakening." Before Whitefield's death, he spoke to millions of Americans, preaching more than eighteen thousand times. He popularized extemporaneous preaching and deliberately engaged people's emotions, a preaching style still considered a standard in evangelical churches.

He held services for slaves in the colonies and is credited with doing more to create a Christian presence within the slave community than any other person in the eighteenth century. While Whitefield is justly criticized for supporting the institution of slavery, he stood against the popular teaching that slaves did not have souls. He warned slave owners that when they prohibited slaves from learning about salvation, they put themselves in danger of receiving God's wrath.

Whitefield was the first person other than members of the British royal family to be well-known among the citizens of all thirteen colonies. He used newspapers, pamphlets, books, and even controversy and criticism from his enemies to draw attention to his work. George Whitefield became an eighteenth-century celebrity and used his fame to spread the gospel. About 80 percent of the American colonists personally heard him speak.

What was it about this itinerant evangelist that prepared him to command such interest? In an age of denominational battles that sometimes led to armed conflict, how was he able to unite Christians of diverse doctrinal persuasions? How did he learn to maintain friendships with people like Ben Franklin who were so different from him, while at the same time never apologizing for his beliefs? The first answers are found in the memories of a family who ran a small English inn.

one

George Whitefield was born on December 16, 1714, in Gloucester, England. He was the youngest son and last child of Thomas and Elizabeth Whitefield. The family lived at the Bell Inn, a prosperous establishment owned by his parents.

The Bell was Gloucester's largest and best inn. It occupied much of a city block in the center of town. The inn rose three floors above the street and included a carriage yard, a stable, and two auditoriums. There were also many guest rooms. A large kitchen served both a well-appointed dining room and a tavern. In addition to the stables attached to the inn, the family owned another stable in a different part of town.

The Bell was a place of business for merchants and craftsmen. Well-known groups of traveling entertainers gave performances on its stages, and it was used for Gloucester social and civic functions as well. Among its

11

regular patrons were people of social prominence and wealth.

As the owners of the Bell Inn, Thomas and Elizabeth Whitefield were well-off, if not quite wealthy. The records of the time show that their tax payments were rather large. They were in a perfect position to jump from the upper middle class to the wealthy, influential, and growing merchant class. The merchant class was defined by success in business, unlike the aristocracy, which was defined by hereditary titles and land ownership.

It would have been natural for George Whitefield's parents to want to reach a higher position in the socially stratified society of their day. Both of their families' backgrounds included wealth, influence, and scholarship. George's father was the son of a wealthy gentleman and grew up on an estate in the lower Severn River valley in the southwestern part of England. Relatives from previous generations of the family had attended Oxford University, and some had gone on to successful careers in the Church of England.

As a young man, Thomas Whitefield worked for a wine merchant in Bristol, but he soon struck out on his own and purchased the Bell Inn at Gloucester. Before Thomas Whitefield left Bristol, he married Elizabeth Edwards. Her family was solidly middle class, and several of her relatives had held important offices in city government.

Though the ownership of a successful inn made the Whitefields respectable members of society, it was seen as only the first step toward financial independence and social prominence. Nor was their financial situation considered secure or independent, since they owned no large estates. Like many in their generation, they were working toward financial freedom.

Then tragedy struck. When George was two years old, his father died. His mother was left to run the Bell Inn by herself, with the help of her children. Suddenly a very difficult situation faced the family. Among them, they had lost a father, a husband, and a business manager. All sorts of tasks and responsibilities had to be quickly reassigned. Some family members had to learn new skills. Inevitably, certain things were left undone and others were poorly supervised. For a few years the inn continued to prosper and the tax rates for the family remained high. But gradually, business declined.

Though information about George's early life is sketchy, it is clear that, like most children in his station of life, he had a nurse. She wasn't a trained medical professional but rather a woman who took care of young children. After George's father died, the nurse stayed on, but it is almost certain that she took on other responsibilities because of the family's situation. About this time George contracted the measles. His nurse wasn't able to watch him closely enough because of her other jobs, and before anyone realized what was happening, the muscles of his left eye were damaged. He could still see, but for the rest of his life that eye turned slightly toward his nose.

No one knows if his father had planned an academic career for George, but it is certain that his mother had that in mind, especially after her husband's death. Entries in George Whitefield's journals indicate that he entered school early. Near the beginning of the first journal, he reported, "My mother was very careful of my education, and always kept me, in my tender years, for which I can never sufficiently thank her, from intermeddling in the least with the public business."

Harry Stout, a recent biographer of Whitefield, believes that, after the death of her husband, Elizabeth Whitefield felt very keenly the threat to her family's financial and social status, and therefore put great pressure on George to recapture that place for them. The most direct route would be for him to earn the distinction of a university education and the honor of a career as a minister in the Church of England.

"George's older brothers helped to run the inn and eventually owned it," Stout observed. "But it was George's mother who exercised the major influence on his childhood. From earliest memory he recalled her singling him out as the son who would make something of himself and the family. As long as she ran the inn she refused to let him work there. Both mother and elder siblings protected George from the world and held out high hopes for him. Inasmuch as earlier generations had made their mark in the Church of England, Elizabeth pointed George in that direction, too. A clerical career would recapture the family's lost distinction and reestablish it on the fringes of English polite society."[1]

George Whitefield certainly felt a great deal of pressure from his mother. It is one of the few things about his early life that he mentions in his journals. He began writing his journals when he was twenty-four years old. They were designed to tell the story of his early spiritual development in hopes that readers would be convinced to make a similar journey. Whitefield's journals were not designed to be a biography and therefore ignore events that didn't pertain to his spiritual life.

So it is stunning to find, at the very beginning of Whitefield's first journal the following entry concerning his mother: "[She] has often told me how she endured fourteen weeks' sickness after she brought me into the world; but was used to say, even when I was an infant, that she expected more comfort from me than any other of her children."

Most people would not consider a mother's expectations for her son's future success to be part of his spiritual journey, but George Whitefield did. Whether his mother intended it or not, her expectations placed a burden on her son that stayed with him for life. George Whitefield felt most things very deeply and was sensitive to the emotional states of those around him. The picture that emerges from the few entries in his journals that speak of his childhood is that of a sensitive, emotional, and sometimes mischievous child.

It is not surprising, given these early impulses, that George soon developed a sense of the dramatic power of everyday life. Nor is it surprising that he soon developed a love of public speaking, public performance in general, and especially the theater.

In the early eighteenth century, England had entered a golden age for playwriting and performance. Traveling groups of actors gave regular performances at the Bell Inn, exposing George to the power of the stage from his earliest days.

Since his family attended local churches regularly, especially the Church of England, preachers gave him some of his earliest examples of more serious and intellectually stimulating public speaking. Young George was soon entertaining family and friends with accurate copies of the prayers, devotional readings, and sermons he heard at church.

By the time he was twelve years old, his abilities in public speaking and acting had been recognized at school as well. "When I was about twelve, I was placed at a school called St. Mary de Crypt, in Gloucester—the last grammar school I ever went to," Whitefield wrote. "Having a good elocution and memory, I was remarked for making speeches before the corporation at their annual visitation."

It is not clear where his earliest schooling took place, but that preparation was solid enough so the masters at St. Mary de Crypt felt no hesitation in setting George up as an example of a model student. One master even selected him, along with some others, for an independent study project.

"During the time of my being at school," Whitefield later recalled, "I was very fond of reading plays, and have kept from school for days together to prepare myself for acting them. My master, seeing how mine and my schoolfellows' vein ran, composed something of this kind for us himself."

Acting was clearly the great love of George's early life. It gave him an outlet for his passionate feelings about life. Whether in the form of public speaking or performing on the stage, performing probably gave him a way of facing the fears of failure and sense of inadequacy that his mother's demands and expectations almost certainly imposed on him. As Harry Stout put it, "Here was an outlet that fit his personality and inborn talents as perfectly as the sermons he mimicked at home. Acting helped him to overcome his fears by 'impersonating' greatness."[2]

Given the brief nature of his comments about his childhood, there is no way to know how deeply George Whitefield studied the art of acting. However, considering his attachment to the stage, it is likely that he would have used any available resources to increase his skills. There were a number of popular and readily available books that discussed how an actor should project emotions through a wide range of facial expressions and carefully contrived body language. The shape of his early preaching certainly showed the unmistakable signs of such influence, however they were acquired.

George may also have poured himself into plays and the other distractions of the theater as things at home changed very much for the worse. About the time George turned eight years old, his mother was drawn into a bad marriage to Capel Longdon, an "ironmonger," or hardware businessman. With no experience in running an inn, Longdon took over. George's older brother, who had grown up in the inn, was forced to apprentice himself to this novice innkeeper. Six years later George's mother ended the marriage. But by that time the reputation of the Bell Inn had been seriously damaged by Longdon's mismanagement.

George's schooling was cut short because the family no longer had the financial resources to pay for his education, and everyone's help was needed to repair the damage that had been done to the family's most important financial asset.

George Whitefield's external circumstances changed drastically during the six Longdon years, but even more damaging was the probable effect on his internal life. Between his mother's demands, his father's absence, and the presence of the corrupt and incompetent Longdon, it became increasingly difficult for George to believe in a secure future for himself. Since much of what children believe about God is closely tied to their relationships with their parents, this extended crisis may have made God seem both distant and demanding to young George Whitefield.

Arnold Dallimore is certainly right when he asserts, "As we look back upon the presence of Longdon in the Whitefield home, we ask what effect it may have had on George. The circumstance of growing up in a fatherless condition, along with the self-consciousness occasioned by his eye affliction, may well have caused feelings of insecurity in so sensitive a child. Without doubt, Longdon afforded him none of the strength and confidence which a child should derive from a father's presence. On the contrary, during the highly formative years from eight to fifteen, George lived in a home which was marred by this unpleasant personality, by increasing financial difficulty, by a sorrowing mother, and finally a broken marriage. He could not but have been affected by such things and we may be sure that the shyness we shall see in him later arose primarily from these boyhood conditions."[3]

After the failure of her marriage, Elizabeth Whitefield turned over the Bell Inn to George's older brother Richard and moved into a small cottage. George soon had a falling out with Richard's wife and ended up living with his mother—sleeping on her floor.

It was while he was experiencing these much reduced circumstances that a new sense of possibilities, and even

18

of destiny, began to develop in him. George had a sense that God would deliver him.

"But God, whose gifts and callings are without repentance, would let nothing pluck me out of His hands," he later wrote in his journals, "though I was continually doing despite to the Spirit of Grace. He saw me with pity and compassion, when lying in my blood. He passed by me; He said unto me, *Live*; and even gave me some foresight of His providing for me.

"One morning, as I was reading a play to my sister, said I, 'Sister, God intends something for me which we know not of. As I have been diligent in business, I believe many would gladly have me for an apprentice, but every way seems to be barred up, so that I think God will provide for me some way or other that we cannot apprehend.' "

Whitefield portrayed this brief conversation as one of the first great turning points in his life. Here was a young man whose future prospects were quite bleak. Yet in spite of everything, he still held out the hope that God would finally rescue him from his condition of abandonment and give him a new future.

A short time later, the way for this rescue became clear. A young student and former schoolmate of George's had rented living quarters from Elizabeth Whitefield for a while. He later stopped by to visit George's mother, and during the conversation explained that he was working his way through Oxford as a servitor at Pembroke College. This job involved acting as a personal servant to wealthy and socially prominent students. In exchange for hard work at menial tasks and a certain amount of social isolation, his expenses were covered. The same option was open to George.

Upon hearing this news, Whitefield reported, "My mother immediately cried out, 'This will do for my son.' Then turning to me, she said, 'Will you go to Oxford, George?' I replied, 'With all my heart.' "

This exchange sounds so much like a scene out of one of George's beloved plays that one wonders if they were the actual words spoken. In any event, both mother and son obviously felt an overwhelming sense of relief.

Now that a way had been found to cover the expenses of an Oxford education, the family could justify the expense of returning George to the school at their parish church, St. Mary de Crypt. He spent the next two years preparing to enter Pembroke College, Oxford, in the fall of 1732.

During those two years, Whitefield's concern for his spiritual life became more consistent and serious. "Being now near the seventeenth year of my age," he recorded in his journals, "I was resolved to prepare myself for the holy Sacrament, which I received on Christmas Day. I began now to be more and more watchful over my thoughts, words, and actions. I kept the following Lent, fasting Wednesday and Friday thirty-six hours together. My evenings, when I had done waiting upon my mother, were generally spent in acts of devotion, reading *Drelincourt on Death*, and other practical books, and I constantly went to public worship twice a day. Being now upper-boy, by God's help I made some reformation amoungst my schoolfellows. I was very diligent in reading and learning the classics, and in studying my Greek Testament, but was not yet convinced of the absolute unlawfulness of playing at cards, and of reading and seeing plays, though I began to have some scruples about it."

Mixed in with much that was good and admirable during these years were two tendencies that would prove extremely destructive in George Whitefield's life. First was the tendency to equate intense religious activity with holiness. Once he began to go more regularly to church, it was soon not enough to go once or twice a week. He was satisfied with nothing less than twice a day.

Second, as his study of the Bible and other academic works increased, the interests and passions of only a few years before began to be seen as enemies. He began equating spiritual discipline with irrational self-denial. Anything that was pleasing to the senses or gave him great joy but did not deal specifically and solely with God had to be ruthlessly eliminated.

These tendencies were to grow more troubling during his time at Oxford. And the social isolation he was about to experience as a servitor only reinforced them.

two

In November 1732 George Whitefield enrolled at
Pembroke College, Oxford University. As he and his
mother had planned, his expenses were covered by
his work as a servitor.

It is hard to know how much about the life of a
servitor George or his mother really understood before
George arrived at Oxford. The colleges that made up
Oxford supported the divisions that existed between
various economic and social classes in Great Britain. At
the top of the social scale at Oxford were the wealthy
and socially prominent gentlemen students. The school
catered to them because they were expected to become
the next generation of leaders—and their influence and
wealth were necessary for the university's survival.

Next came the common students who had enough
money to pay their own way but who lacked the connections of the gentlemen students. They received much

less attention. Misbehavior that would be tolerated from gentlemen was not tolerated from the common students.

At the bottom were the servitors, who were charity cases. "The servitor's work was hard and often demeaning," Harry Stout explains. "When not acting as errand boys for gentlemen, they were often required to perform such degrading tasks as cleaning clothes and rooms and serving at parties. They also worked for the college master and assumed the unenviable task of checking rooms at night and reporting students who were not in their quarters. This understandably did not win friends among the gentlemen students, who would retaliate by going 'hunting.' Late at night the servitors would be chased through the college by angry gentlemen clanging pots and candlesticks in imitation of a fox hunt. Such experiences bred a spirit of resentment, anger, and inferiority."[1]

One servitor would work with three or four gentlemen students. His duties might include waking them in the morning, blacking their shoes, and even doing their homework. The inferior status of the servitors continued after they completed their duties. They were required to wear to classes a different academic gown than those worn by their fellow students. It was inappropriate for gentlemen or even common students to be seen in public with a servitor. Though close friendships sometimes developed, they were kept carefully private.

Though servitors were free to attend classes with other students, they were kept from other college activities. Instead of joining the other students in weekly debates and religious services, servitors were required to hold their own. The inferior status of servitors was so painful that many young men chose to leave school rather than live with it.

At least George had been prepared for the actual work of a servitor by his years helping out at the Bell Inn. He soon gained a reputation as one of the best servitors in Pembroke College.

All students at Oxford were assigned a tutor to guide their education. The quality of education received at the university was largely dependent on the commitment and qualifications of that person. Fortunately, Whitefield had a very good one. His name apparently was George Henry Rooke, and he held a doctor's degree, something that was much more unusual in the eighteenth century than it is today.

Whitefield recorded in his journal some telling comments about how George Rooke responded to Whitefield's spiritual disciplines and looked after his well-being. "My tutor, being a moderate man, did not oppose me much, but thought, I believe, that I went a little too far. He lent me books, gave me money, visited me, and furnished me with a physician when sick. In short, he behaved in all respects like a father; and I trust God will remember him for good, in answer to the many prayers I have put up in his behalf."

That his tutor thought he went "a little too far" with his spiritual exercises is probably an understatement. At first, Whitefield was content to simply expand the rigorous schedule of spiritual activity that he had followed in preparation for Oxford. He continued to read the Bible frequently, but now his understanding of holiness was also shaped by a series of devotional and theological books.

One author in particular was important to his spiritual growth at this time. "Before I went to the University, I met with Mr. Law's *Serious Call to a Devout Life*," Whitefield explained, "but had not then money to purchase it. Soon after my coming up to the University, seeing a small edition of it in a friend's hand, I soon procured it. God worked powerfully upon my soul, as he has since upon many others, by that and his other excellent treatise upon *Christian Perfection*."

William Law's *A Serious Call to a Devout and Holy Life*, which had been published only four years before Whitefield entered Oxford, was just beginning its long influence on spiritual disciplines. It prompted Whitefield to establish a new routine of devotional activities. "I now began to pray and sing psalms thrice every day, besides morning and evening, and to fast every Friday, and to receive the Sacrament at a parish church near our college, and at the castle, where the despised Methodists used to receive once a month."

This was but one of several strategies he used to cope with the difficulties of being both a servitor and a first-year student at an elite university. He also threw himself into his studies with passionate intensity. Whitefield did not want to waste the educational opportunity he had been given, because he believed it had come directly from God. He was appalled by much of the behavior he saw around him. "It has often grieved my soul to see so many young students spending their substance in extravagant living," he wrote, "and thereby entirely unfitting themselves for the prosecution of their studies."

During the first few months of his university career, Whitefield separated himself from those around him who were engaged in what he considered frivolous or immoral behavior. One incident recorded in his first journal is particularly striking. "I had not been long at the University, before I found the benefit of the foundation I had laid in the country for a holy life. I was quickly solicited to join in their excess of riot with several who lay in the same room. God, in answer to prayers before put up, gave me grace to withstand them; and once in particular, it being cold, my limbs were so benumbed by sitting alone in my study, because I would not go out amongst them, that I could scarce sleep all night. But I soon found the benefit of not yielding: for when they perceived they could not prevail, they let me alone as a singular odd fellow."

Whitefield does not specify what "excess of riot" he observed, but Oxford at this time had its share of coarse language, violent pranks, drunken parties, and sexual immorality. He was certainly justified in fearing for his spiritual health, but his response seems excessive and somewhat prideful. His very next journal entry shows his determination to give up what had been a source of great pleasure to this point.

"All this while I was not fully satisfied of the sin of playing at cards and reading plays, till God upon a fast-day was pleased to convince me. For, taking a play, to read a passage out of it to a friend, God struck my heart with such power, that I was obliged to lay it down again; and, blessed be His Name, I have not read any such book since."

It may seem odd to reject all plays at face value. But in the first decades of the eighteenth century, the stage and those who made their living through dramatic presentations were often the subject of vitriolic attacks from

Christian leaders. Some plays contained foul language and grossly immoral situations. In others, dishonest characters were presented as heroes, and decent people were held up to ridicule. Christian leaders were sometimes portrayed as sly manipulators of everyone around them. Christian characters often appeared as greedy, drunken, gluttonous, or sexually perverse.

But many plays were designed to uncover social ills so that solutions could be found for them. Religious corruption occupied a special place in many of these stories because the memory of Puritan oppression under Oliver Cromwell in the mid-seventeenth century was still vividly alive in the minds of many of the English. They worried that religious oppression would return. Because of this, anyone who showed too much religious zeal or "enthusiasm" was looked upon as potentially dangerous.

George Whitefield's spiritual development was deeply influenced by the writings of Puritan thinkers and other nonconformists from the seventeenth century, so it is not surprising that he also picked up their anti-drama views. His choice to renounce plays also fits in well with the developing beliefs of most British and American evangelicals in the eighteenth century.

But for Whitefield, with his natural feeling for the dramatic flow of daily life, this decision created a terrible internal conflict. The real problem was not the plays themselves but the feelings of passion they stirred up in him. He could not reconcile his passionate nature with what he increasingly saw as the demand of the gospel that passions of any kind should be directed solely toward God.

Whitefield's growing fear of "ungodly" passions and

his growing need for "godly" passion to fill the emotional void left by the choking off of his normal emotional life would have serious consequences throughout his life. But the short-term effect was to release tremendous emotional energy into his religious life. The search for God and the pursuit of holiness became Whitefield's only emotional or dramatic outlet. Without realizing what he was doing, George Whitefield was becoming the sole player in a one act religious drama of his own creation. Before the end of his second year at Oxford, the spiritual crisis it unleashed would very nearly kill him.

As Whitefield slowly shaped his response to the environment he found at Oxford, he gradually isolated himself from many of the other students. However, sometime during the spring or summer of 1733, his disciplined lifestyle and concern for godliness brought him to the attention of fellow student Charles Wesley, who invited him to breakfast. Their meeting probably occurred in August or September 1733.

Charles Wesley was breaking the rules about contact with servitors, so it is not surprising to find Whitefield remembering that first meeting by the following entry in his journal: "I thankfully embraced the opportunity; and, blessed be God! it was one of the most profitable visits I ever made in my life. My soul, at that time, was athirst for some spiritual friends to lift up my hands when they hung down, and to strengthen my feeble knees."

Before he had ever arrived at Pembroke College, Whitefield had already heard of the small group of ten to twenty men from several colleges at Oxford University who were derisively referred to as the "Holy Club," "Bible

Moths," or the "Methodists," among other, less flattering, names.

Under the leadership of John and Charles Wesley, group members organized their lives around a whole series of shared disciplines. They got up early in the morning so that they could begin their days with prayer, Bible reading, the reading of Christian books, and the examination of their lives. Much of their study was conducted at a very rigorous academic level. For example, when they read, studied, or discussed the New Testament, it was usually the Greek New Testament they were using.

They worked hard to organize all their time during the day and to use it wisely. At night they recorded their successes and failures in a diary. These accounts would be shared with other members of the group to create accountability. This methodical living was the origin of the term *methodist*.

Attendance at church was very important to them. They spent time on Saturday preparing for Sunday services so that they could take communion every Sunday with a clear conscience. They also fasted twice a week.

In order to help those less fortunate than themselves, the "methodists" regularly visited Oxford's prisons, where they provided food, clothing, and spiritual counsel to the inmates. They also worked to make life better for the inmates' families, who were often trapped in poverty. Many poor people in and around Oxford received spiritual and monetary help from the methodists.

The Wesleys and their followers believed that these disciplined actions of religious devotion and charity would help them draw closer to Christ and make them more acceptable to God.

George Whitefield was strongly drawn to these men. He records in his journal, "I now began, like them, to live by rule, and to pick up the very fragments of my time, that not a moment of it might be lost. Whether I ate or drank, or whatsoever I did, I endeavoured to do all to the glory of God."

Though it is unlikely that Whitefield consciously understood what he was doing, he and the other methodists were seeking to create a unique place for themselves at Oxford and in the larger world. The gentlemen students had a place by right of birth, and the common students one by right of purchase, but the evangelical students, whatever their social status, found it difficult to function within those larger groups or to influence them in significant ways. John and Charles Wesley were paying students, whose family background nearly allowed them to claim the title of "gentlemen," so their isolation was somewhat less than Whitefield's, but they still sought the companionship, safety, and discipline of the methodist counterculture. The isolation Whitefield faced as a servitor was even more severe, and his need for an accepting group was even greater.

Harry Stout is right to observe, "On a personal level, methodism offered these alienated students an element of control and meaning in a rapidly changing world. Their strict discipline spoke to the enduring Protestant need to discover meaning in the transaction between God and the self, and to impose that discipline on a chaotic world. If the world ignored or reviled them, they would ignore the world and appeal to a higher destiny. In Whitefield, the powerful inclination toward spiritual fame coincided with a rebellious methodist impetus against the world and its mores. As the eighteenth-century theater poked fun at elite morality and manners on the English stage, so methodism assaulted polite pastimes and preoccupations from the pulpit. Each in its own way was a powerful countercul-ture, standing apart from traditional order and proud of its defiance."[2]

Whitefield's involvement with the methodists contin-ued, along with his pursuit of his studies at Oxford, with-out much interruption until the fall of 1734. There is every reason to believe that Whitefield's involvement with Charles, John, and the others actually improved his commitment to his college work because John Wesley considered disciplined scholarship to be a Christian virtue.

All of this began to change in the last months of 1734. George Whitefield got a copy of *The Life of God in the Soul of Man* by Henry Scougal. The writings of this Scots-man from the seventeenth century convinced Whitefield that "I must be born again, or be damned."

This opened a whole new world of spiritual reality for Whitefield. Suddenly, it dawned on him that following Christ could be a matter of internal transformation, with God doing some of the work—that "true religion is a union of the soul with God, and Christ formed within us," in Scougal's words. Whitefield's response, as he recorded it in a sermon preached years later, seems quite simple: "A ray of Divine light was instantaneously darted in upon my soul, and from that moment, but not till then, did I know that I must become a new creature."

But George Whitefield had some distance to go before he could understand that he needed to surrender his life simply and personally to Christ. And he had even further to go before he would realize that salvation was the work of God in his life, not the result of his own pursuit of holiness. That journey was to be filled with pain, suffering, and even a brush with death.

Whitefield's need for dramatic experiences in his life, combined with the methodist understanding of holiness, added to the difficulty of this journey. For all their well-intentioned religious activity, these English pietists had lost touch with one of the most important ideas of the Protestant Reformation—that salvation came through faith, not by way of works.

Believing that he had to go out and find a strategy for uniting his soul with God and forming Christ within himself by his own efforts, Whitefield began an agonizing, months-long search for this state of holiness. His quest began with the idea of healthy self-discipline but quickly led him to a series of increasingly severe acts of self-denial.

It is difficult to determine exactly how these patterns developed because Whitefield's journal is not clear on these matters. His writings communicate more about the raw emotions of these experiences than about the specific order of the events. However, several patterns of behavior can be identified, and it is likely that they developed together over a period of months rather than by one simply following another in strict chronological order.

Whitefield first began to approach his religious activities with even more vigor than in the past, and this caused him to get less sleep. He cut himself off from relationships that did not directly contribute to his spiritual quest, even though this attitude apparently alienated some of the gentlemen students who had previously been glad to have him as their servitor.

He began to abuse his body by eating less and restricting his diet to "the worst sort of food." In order to increase the perceived spiritual virtue of this choice, he gave away to the poor the money he had saved.

Not surprisingly, the loss of sleep and change in diet created a gradual state of emotional vulnerability and instability. So he found himself overwhelmed with imagined and irrational fears. He wrote, "All power of meditating, or even thinking, was taken from me. My memory quite failed me. My whole soul was barren and dry, and I could fancy myself to be like nothing so much as a man locked up in iron armour."

In another place, he recorded this incredible situation: "At this time, Satan used to terrify me much, and threatened to punish me if I discovered his wiles. It being my duty, as servitor, in my turn to knock at the gentlemen's rooms by ten at night, to see who were in their rooms, I thought the Devil would appear to me every stair I went up. And he so troubled me when I lay down to rest, that for some weeks I scarce slept above three hours at a time."

He wore old clothes and dirty shoes and liked to go about on campus without a powdered wig, all to make his condition as a penitent visible for everyone to see. He tried new devotional disciplines but claimed Satan was driving him to extremes that destroyed many of the practices he had learned from the methodists, such as keeping a spiritual diary, following prescribed devotional readings, using written prayers, and visiting the poor.

His academic studies collapsed, and his tutor became

seriously concerned that Whitefield had lost his mind. He even began to withdraw from his methodist friends, until both Charles and John Wesley took him aside and convinced him to go back to something like a reasonable devotional life.

Two letters Whitefield wrote to friends, one in early December 1734 and the other in late February 1735, show something of the legalistic trap he had fallen into and the difficulties he was having even considering that salvation "by faith alone" was an option.

In the first letter he said, "The book which I have sent to my brother and would recommend to you and all my Gloucester friends, will soon convince you how dangerous it is to be a lukewarm Christian, and that there is nothing to be done without breaking from the world, denying ourselves daily, taking up our cross, and following Jesus Christ. These things may seem a little terrible at first; but, believe me, mortification itself, when once practised, is the greatest pleasure in the world."

His second letter, referring to Scougal's *The Life of God in the Soul of Man,* stated, "[It] will inform you what true religion is, and by what means you may attain it; as, likewise, how wretchedly most people err in their sentiments about it, who suppose it to be nothing else but a mere model of outward performances, without ever considering that all our corrupt passions must be subdued, and a complex habit of virtues, such as meekness, lowliness, faith, hope, and the love of God and of man, be implanted in their room, before we can have the least title to enter into the kingdom of God."

Even the concern and intervention of the Wesleys could not keep Whitefield from falling back into self-abuse during Lent in the early spring of 1735. He used certain methodist practices as an excuse for his excesses. "Soon after this, the holy season of Lent came on," he wrote in his journal, "which our friends kept very strictly, eating no flesh during the six weeks, except on Saturdays also, and ate nothing on the other days, except on Sunday, but sage-tea without sugar, and coarse bread. I constantly walked out in the cold mornings till part of one of my hands was quite black. This, with my continued abstinence, and inward conflicts, at length so emaciated my body, that, at Passion-week, finding I could scarce creep upstairs, I was obliged to inform my kind tutor of my condition, who immediately sent for a physician to me."

He was sick and mostly confined to bed for seven weeks. During this time he attempted to continue his reading and prayer but was forced to stop abusing his body. Shortly after Easter, in a state of utter exhaustion and nearly complete spiritual despair, Whitefield cast himself on the mercy of God, and "a full assurance of faith broke in upon my disconsolate soul!"

George Whitefield had finally found the peace with God that had eluded him for so long. He would always consider this the pivotal moment of his life and would often repeat the story in sermons. The ending usually went something like this: "I know the place! It may be superstitious, perhaps, but whenever I go to Oxford I cannot help running to that place where Jesus Christ first revealed himself to me and gave me the new birth."

George Whitefield had discovered the new birth, and now he would proclaim that discovery to all who would listen—until it shook the foundations of his world.

three

George Whitefield was ecstatic about his conversion experience, and he was quick to let as many people know about it as his fragile health would allow. His family and friends were relieved to see that his sense of despair had finally lifted. Many at Oxford had begun to fear for his life. Two years before, a respected young methodist named William Morgan had faced a similar period of spiritual agony. The physical stresses of his unresolved struggle had led to insanity and death.

Whitefield soon understood that his weakened physical condition would not allow him to remain at Oxford. He returned to Gloucester in the early summer of 1735 to recuperate. Whitefield did not have any money, and he had debts from his last months at Oxford. Gabriel Harris, a prominent bookseller, gave Whitefield a place to stay. The whole Harris family was kind to George, and their acceptance encouraged others to welcome and support him as well.

George immediately found that some in Gloucester wanted him to give up his disciplined lifestyle of church attendance, personal devotions, methodist society commitments, and charity work. He resisted their suggestions, continuing to attend church regularly.

His reading and study began to connect him with the basic theology of the Protestant Reformers and started him down the path to discovering what he came to call "the doctrines of grace." While his theology wasn't completely formed, he believed that salvation by faith was a work that God accomplished in the life of the believer. Because it was God's work, it was permanent.

God no longer seemed far off and threatening to Whitefield. Prayer became a great joy for him. One of the things Whitefield prayed about often was the need for some companions who were serious about developing their spiritual lives. "Not long after," he recorded in his journal, "God made me instrumental to awaken several young persons, who soon formed themselves into a little Society, and had quickly the honour of being despised at Gloucester, as we had been before them at Oxford."

Whitefield was quite excited about this group. The agenda for the meetings was adapted from the Holy Club at Oxford. The group sang, read the Bible, and prayed. Whitefield then read from a theological work or a practical book on Christian living. He would "exhort" the group for anywhere from a few minutes to a couple of hours. At other times during the week, both Whitefield and the members of the society worked with the poor or those in prison.

This group is historically significant because it was the first permanent methodist society. The group of believers in Gloucester would grow and change over the years, but it would always be part of Whitefield's life and ministry.

Whitefield was not content to simply build up the new methodist society and quietly pursue charity work. When a traveling group of actors came to Gloucester (and probably performed at the Bell Inn, which was still owned by his family), Whitefield persuaded a local newspaper to print a six-part denunciation of the stage and plays.

Both the positive example of his life and his outspoken opposition to the theater convinced many that, whether they agreed with him or not, George Whitefield's life had changed. But George Whitefield was not yet convinced that God wanted him to enter the Christian ministry. The idea of becoming a minister in the Church of England had been a part of his life since he was a child. Now, however, he found himself afraid of the responsibilities such a position included. Even more, he feared that pride might overwhelm him and separate him from God if his preaching proved popular. In his later sermon, "The Good Shepherd," Whitefield reflected on this time:

> *God alone knows how deep a concern entering the ministry and preaching was to me. I have prayed a thousand times, till the sweat has dropped from my face like rain, that God. . .would not let me enter the Church before he called me and thrust me into his work.*

*I remember once in Gloucester, I know the
room. . .the bedside and the floor upon which I
have lain prostrate, I said, Lord, I cannot go; I
shall be puffed up with pride and fall into the
snare of the devil.*

George Whitefield wanted a specific, measurable indi-
cation from God that he should pursue a career in the
church. The encouragement of his bishop, Dr. Benson,
didn't seem quite dramatic enough to be considered a
divine commission. So Whitefield asked God to solve his
very real financial problems. When more than enough
money came in to remove his indebtedness, he was convinced it was time to return to school, finish his education,
and prepare for ordination in the Church of England.

Whitefield returned to Oxford in March 1736 and prepared for his most important undergraduate examination. It would all but complete the required work for his
bachelor's degree. Several weeks of disciplined study
soon led to success, and the last obstacle to his ordination was removed.

On the morning of Sunday, June 20, 1736, George
Whitefield was ordained a deacon in the Church of England at Gloucester Cathedral. That afternoon he performed
his first official ministerial functions by reading prayers
to prisoners.

Seven days later he preached his first sermon as an
ordained minister. The title of the sermon was "The
Nature and Necessity of Society in General and Religious
Society in Particular." It was a topic of special relevance
to Whitefield, who had so often felt separated from both

God and other people.

As he walked to the pulpit, he looked both very young and very nervous. But the nervousness began to ease as he became caught up in a sense of God's power and presence. It was an extraordinary moment for him. Finally, his sense of the drama of life and his need to express it were linked with the certainty that God approved of these passions and was even the driving force behind them.

The result was a stunning piece of religious theater and a great success in terms of its impact on the congregation. Whitefield's record of the event in his diary tells us clearly how much this day meant to him:

> *Curiosity, as you may easily guess, drew a large congregation. The sight at first a little awed me, but I was comforted with a heartfelt sense of the Divine presence and soon found the unspeakable advantage of having been accustomed to public speaking when a boy at school, and of exhorting and teaching the prisoners and poor people at their private houses whilst at the University. By these means I was kept from being daunted over-much.*
>
> *As I proceeded, I perceived the fire kindled, till at last, though so young and amidst a crowd of those who knew me in my infant childish days, I trust I was enabled to speak with some degree of gospel authority. Some few mocked, but most for the present seemed struck, and I have since heard that a complaint has been made to the Bishop that I drove fifteen mad the first sermon. The worthy Prelate, as I am*

*informed, wished that the madness might not be
forgotten before next Sunday.*

At the end of June George Whitefield returned to
Oxford to receive his bachelor's degree and to pursue
graduate studies. He also found himself the leader of the
Holy Club because both of the Wesleys had gone to the
colony of Georgia the previous year as missionaries.

His enjoyment of university life was interrupted in early
August by a request from the Reverend Thomas
Broughton that he come to London and preach. This
friend of Whitefield's was the well-known minister of
the Chapel of the Tower of London, a man who was
well-connected to many people of social prominence
and political power. He also had influence with many
leaders in the hierarchy of the Church of England.

Whitefield spent two months in London, and word
of the dramatic preaching style of the "boy parson" drew
a steady stream of both the influential and the simply
curious. Many who later became his strongest supporters
first heard of him during this time. He also received a letter from John Wesley, begging for his help in Georgia.

Near the beginning of October, Whitefield returned
to Oxford, not realizing that the whole direction of his
life was about to change. Within a few weeks, he was
offered a permanent position in London by the bishop
himself. Later, in November, he received a second letter
from John Wesley, again asking him to come to Georgia.
Wesley warned that the whole work of God there might
collapse for lack of workers.

During that winter Whitefield decided to go to

41

Georgia. He believed that the rigors of a barely tamed land would be a better place than London to gain important practical experience and spiritual maturity.

At the beginning of 1737, Whitefield left Oxford and traveled to Gloucester and then Bristol to inform his friends, family members, and supporters of his decision. He was asked to conduct services in both cities, and found the Bristol crowds particularly large and enthusiastic. He even made a quick trip to nearby Bath, at that time England's most fashionable resort, where he preached twice.

In the early part of February, he traveled to London, intending to find passage as quickly as possible to America. There he was introduced to General James Oglethorpe, the founder of Georgia, who said he was expecting to leave for the colony shortly and specifically requested that Whitefield sail with him.

During several weeks of waiting in London, Whitefield received many requests to preach and accepted one from the Reverend Sampson Harris of the Gloucestershire village of Stonehouse. When he arrived there in May, he found Harris's congregation spiritually well cared for and could report, "I followed his good example, and found great freedom and assistance given me both in my public and private administrations. . . . Neither church nor house could contain the people that came."

Once again, part of the reason for his success was his willingness to express his passionate love for God. On May 23 Whitefield returned to Bristol. He threw himself into the work with his characteristic enthusiasm, and the response was overwhelming.

"I preached, as usual, about five times a week," he

wrote, "but the congregations grew, if possible, larger and larger. It was wonderful to see how the people hung upon the rails of the organ loft, climbed upon the leads of the church, and made the church itself so hot with their breath, that the steam would fall from the pillars like drops of rain. Sometimes, almost as many would go away, for want of room, as came in; and it was with great difficulty that I got into the desk, to read prayers or preach. Persons of all denominations flocked to hear. Persons of all ranks, not only publicly attended my ministry, but gave me private invitations to their houses." The tremendous response to Whitefield's preaching on the new birth and the need for practical holiness continued for most of the remainder of 1737.

In December George Whitefield found that Governor Oglethorpe was still not ready to sail, but a group of soldiers being sent to defend the colony from the Spanish was ready to leave. He decided to sail with the soldiers. Whitefield did not travel alone. Nor did he go without a carefully thought out plan.

During the past year, Whitefield had talked with many people, including Governor Oglethorpe, about the situation in Georgia. He had also received letters from Charles Wesley that described many of the problems that he would face in trying to preach the gospel in the colony.

Though introducing people to the new birth was Whitefield's basic reason for making this trip, he also wanted to show them the love of God in a more tangible way, just as he had in his work with the poor and the prisoners while he was at Oxford. Wesley's letters gave him an idea of how to do this. It was clear to him that this newly settled and sparsely populated colony had an unusually large number of very poor people. They were struggling just to survive.

These people needed many basic supplies, and he wanted to provide them with items that would make their lives easier. For one thing, there was a great need for schools. Meanwhile, an unusually large number of children were orphans, and many adults familiar with the colony felt there was an urgent need to create a facility to meet the orphans' needs.

Whitefield's supplies included a complete stock of basic clothing. He also obtained many basic household provisions such as oatmeal, cheese, and spices. Added to these was a supply of common medicines. Tools such as claw hammers, shovels, axes, and nails were purchased, along with powder, shot, and gun flints.

Since his plans included new educational opportunities, he added paper and quill pens, as well as pen-knives for maintaining the quills. He selected a large number of books on religious subjects, as well as a few books on practical subjects, such as farming and caring for livestock.

Someone would have to oversee the distribution of all these supplies once they reached Georgia. Daily housekeeping needed to be done, transportation arranged for, and schedules maintained. An ever-increasing volume of correspondence from supporters had to be answered. Schools needed to be started, and the many details involved with founding an orphanage had to be worked out.

To help him with the complex task he had undertaken, George Whitefield chose five young men to make the journey with him. The group included two teachers, two servants, and one personal assistant—James Habersham.

Habersham was particularly important since he was to become the superintendent of the orphanage.

On Friday, December 30, 1737, George Whitefield said his last good-byes to many of his supporters, and he and his fellow workers boarded the *Whitaker*. Whitefield and his companions did not wait for their ship to leave British waters before they began caring for both the practical and spiritual needs of those on board. On their second day out, they held a public prayer service on the open deck. Whitefield followed it with a sermon. He recorded in his journal that he believed the people were somewhat moved.

The actual response was not as positive as he might have hoped. Dr. John Gillies, who assembled one of the earliest and most complete collections of Whitefield's letters, sermons, and other papers, described the situation during the first few days this way: "The captains, both of the soldiers and sailors, with the surgeon and a young cadet, gave him soon to understand that they looked on him as an impostor, and for a while treated him as such. The first Lord's Day one of them played on the hautboy [oboe] and nothing was to be seen but cards, and little heard but cursing and swearing."

Whitefield quickly changed tactics in an effort to "catch them with holy guile." Both he and others in his party began to visit their shipmates as the *Whitaker* made its slow way down the Thames toward the English Channel. Sickness broke out because of the crowded conditions, so they passed out remedies from the supplies they had brought with them.

Whitefield continued to conduct very short prayer services each morning and evening, but he did not preach again for a while. He also spent time with the officers, seamen, soldiers, and other passengers, getting to know them and interjecting Christian ideas into these conversations as opportunities presented themselves. He asked James Habersham to instruct the children on board in reading, and invited any of the soldiers or sailors who could not yet read to join them.

By January 9 the *Whitaker* dropped anchor at Margate. Whitefield learned that John Wesley had just returned from Georgia after a miserable experience and was headed for London. Wesley sent a note to his former Oxford colleague, strongly advising him not to go to Georgia. Whitefield sent back a note giving his reasons for continuing.

The *Whitaker* left British waters on February 2, 1738. It was already carrying a full crew, roughly one hundred soldiers, and about thirty civilian passengers, and was set to pick up more soldiers at Gibraltar. Two other British ships that were also transporting troops to Georgia would accompany it.

The more time Whitefield spent with the ship's officers, the more favorable their assessment of him became. About the time the *Whitaker* and her escorts were making their way out of the English Channel, Whitefield was allowed to preach to the ship's company on a regular basis.

Most members of the ship's company began attending morning or evening services once a day, many read the Bible more regularly, and virtually everyone became involved in religious studies or conversations of some kind. On the journey from Gibraltar to Georgia this pattern continued, with George Whitefield sometimes preaching to groups of people gathered on the decks of all three ships as they sailed side by side.

On May 7, 1738, four months after leaving England, the *Whitaker* and her sister ships reached Savannah, Georgia. At the time, Savannah was little more than a cleared area in the woods, where perhaps a hundred houses stood. With the addition of the soldiers and civilian passengers on the three English ships, the population of the entire colony of Georgia was not more than one thousand.

Whitefield and his five companions quickly set out to establish the same kind of devotional disciplines and strict personal habits that had characterized the Holy Club at Oxford. At the same time, they were very careful not to let their highly structured personal lives translate into harsh or judgmental treatment of those around them.

As they had done on board ship, Whitefield and his associates passed out needed food, medicine, and other supplies. Whitefield soon found that America was not as bad as he had expected. Writing to the Harrises at Gloucester, he could say, "America is not so horrid a place as it is represented to be. The heat of the weather, lying on the ground, etc., are mere painted lions in the way, and to a soul filled with divine love are not worth mentioning. . . . As to my ministerial office, God (such is His goodness) sets His seal to it here as at other places. . . . I visit from house to house, catechise, read prayers twice and expound the two second lessons every day; read to a houseful of people three times a week; expound the two lessons at five in the morning, read prayers and preach twice, and expound the catechism to servants, etc., at seven in the evening every Sunday."

The secretary of the colony, Colonel William Stephens,

spoke for most of the people who came in contact with George Whitefield when he recorded in his official journal on July 2, 1738: "Mr. Whitefield gains more and more on the affections of the people, by his labour and assiduity in the performance of divine offices; to which an open and easy deportment, without show of austerity, or singularity of behaviour in conversation, contribute not little."

The devastating reality of Georgia's huge orphan population struck Whitefield repeatedly as he traveled about from one small settlement to another. He soon decided it was essential to cut short his work in order to return to England and raise money for a much-needed orphanage.

At the last service Whitefield held before leaving, Colonel Stephens reported that the "congregation was so crowded that a great many stood without the doors, and under the windows to hear him, pleased with nothing more than the assurances he gave of his intention to return to them as soon as possible."

The return voyage began in early September, with great hope for a speedy passage, but Whitefield's ship encountered a terrible storm that left it severely damaged. By the time it reached landfall on the western coast of Ireland two months later, Whitefield was weak and ill.

Several religious and governmental leaders in Ireland offered the young preacher lodging so that he could recover. Whitefield, however, was determined to return to England as quickly as possible. By the end of November, George Whitefield was back in England. And he knew that another storm awaited him there.

four

When George Whitefield arrived in London in December 1738, he was met with news both good and bad. The good news was that, during his absence, John and Charles Wesley had developed a close relationship with a group of Moravians. Through that association, the brothers had come to personal faith in Jesus Christ. They were both convinced that justification was through faith alone, rather than something to be earned by good deeds.

No records exist indicating that George Whitefield had ever preached the doctrine of justification by faith up to this point. But now, not only the Moravians but also his friends the Wesley brothers were preaching it at every turn. Although surprised, Whitefield did not disagree with the teaching. In his journal on December 10, he wrote, "The old doctrine about Justification by Faith only, I found much revived. . . . And who dare assert that we are not justified in the sight of God merely by an act of faith in Jesus Christ, without any regard to works past, present, or to come?"

The bad news was that London churches were no longer enthralled by the preaching of George Whitefield. To begin with, many leaders within the Church of England were deeply offended by the Wesley brothers' association with the Moravians. People in some quarters probably held Whitefield's close friendship with the Wesleys against him.

Adding to these people's reservations was what they read in Whitefield's journals and nine of his sermons, which had been published by friends of Whitefield during his absence from England. His message of the new birth received a great deal of attention—not all of it good. Many church officials believed anyone who taught about the new birth to be a methodist and a troublemaker.

More disturbing, however, was that because no one had edited the journals, in many places Whitefield came across as incredibly egotistical and dangerously unbalanced. One person published a thirty-two-page pamphlet titled "Remarks on the Reverend Mr. Whitefield's Journal. Wherein his many Inconsistencies are pointed out, and his Tenets considered. The whole shewing the dangerous tendency of his Doctrine. Addressed to the Religious Societies." The religious societies at whom the pamphlet was targeted were among the groups that had most enthusiastically supported Whitefield before he left for Georgia.

So when he arrived in London, expecting churches to be as open to him as they had been the year before, George Whitefield was in for a shock. Only two churches in all of London allowed him to speak in their pulpits.

Never one to give up easily, Whitefield devised a strategy. First, at the beginning of 1739, he approached Bishop Benson, who had enthusiastically ordained him as a deacon, and asked to be ordained a priest in the Church of England. Familiar with Whitefield's journals, the bishop had reservations, but he agreed to the ordination, assigning Whitefield to Georgia with responsibility for the orphanage and the surrounding parish. Bishop Benson may have been hoping that Whitefield would spend most of his time on another continent, making him less likely to stir up trouble within English churches. But Whitefield fully intended to remain in England for the time being. He knew that once he had secured his ordination and his "living," as the assignment was termed, he could ask to speak about the orphanage in any of London's churches.

In a letter, the bishop made it clear that he had ordained Whitefield in part as a favor to the Earl of Huntingdon and his wife. "I hope this will give some satisfaction to my lady," the bishop wrote to the earl, "and that she will not have occasion to find fault with your lordship's old tutor. *Though mistaken on some points,* I think Mr. Whitefield a very pious, well-meaning young man, with good abilities and great zeal."

The Countess of Huntingdon was to be an important benefactor in George Whitefield's life. A follower of methodist teachings herself, she devoted her time, money, and social power to helping methodist ministers find avenues for preaching, particularly to her friends in the aristocracy. She often invited Whitefield and other young preachers whose teachings she endorsed to speak to her guests. The guests, not willing to offend such an influential woman, sat through the sermons regardless of what they personally thought of the message or the messengers.

One of the more tart responses the Countess of Huntingdon received to an invitation to hear one of these sermons came from the Duchess of Buckingham, who had loose ties to the royal family. "I thank your ladyship for the information concerning the Methodist preachers," she wrote. "Their doctrines are most repulsive, and strongly tinctured with impertinence and disrespect towards their superiors, in perpetually endeavouring to level all ranks, and do away with all distinctions. It is monstrous to be told that you have a heart as sinful as the common wretches that crawl on the earth. This is highly offensive and insulting; and I cannot but wonder that your ladyship should relish any sentiments so much at variance with high rank and good breeding. However, I shall be most happy to accept your kind offer of accompanying me to hear your favourite preacher, and shall wait your arrival."

Whitefield was happy to have such opportunities to share the gospel with members of the aristocracy, yet he wanted his message to have a broader audience. He did not expect the rigid barriers between social classes and between races to disappear, but he earnestly believed that everyone was a sinner—no matter what social circle they were born into—and that the gospel should be available to any person.

With the churches resistant to letting him speak, George Whitefield was thinking of other options. One possibility was to preach in fields, taverns, and other public places. As a child, he'd seen acting troupes who asked permission to perform at his parents' inn and vendors who wanted to hawk their wares near it. He also was aware of Howell Harris, a young methodist minister who preached to crowds gathered in open fields. Whitefield began a correspondence with Harris during this time, and the two men encouraged each other over the next several years.

Before Whitefield began speaking in public places, however, the twenty-four-year-old preacher had to be sure that he wouldn't be allowed to preach in the churches. Some people believe that what happened next was the result of youth and ignorance. Others think it was an intentional act on Whitefield's part and that he didn't care how it struck people. Still others hold that the act was intentional, but that because of Whitefield's inexperience he didn't understand the extent of the trouble it would cause.

Whether knowingly or not, Whitefield substituted at a church in London when the regular preacher had already arranged for another man to fill the pulpit. In the minds of many church leaders, this action seemed to confirm the arrogance they had perceived in his journals. Accounts of the incident were published widely in the press. When Whitefield then traveled to Bath and asked to speak in what was, with the exception of the cathedral, the finest church in the area, he was generally perceived to have overstepped his bounds. Even his staunchest defenders admit that such a request from a young priest assigned to an obscure parish in an American colony was out of line. The fact that Whitefield wouldn't take no for an answer and instead sought approval from two other people, including the dean of the cathedral, did nothing to improve the situation.

For his part, Whitefield took the refusal of the church officials to let him preach as evidence that he should use public places as a forum for his message. On February 17, 1739, he began a six-week outdoor campaign in southwest England. Never one to take the easy way, he began his speaking in the Kingswood mining district near Bristol. Men, women, and children worked long hours in the coal pits that covered the countryside. Their lives were shorter than average, and many people in England considered them to be among the most desperate individuals in the nation.

Whitefield asked his friend William Seward to accompany him. Seward came from a wealthy family, but had embraced methodism. After the two men had received a formal refusal to use the local church, they rode in Seward's coach through town, announcing that a sermon would be preached that evening out in the fields on Hanham Mount. People were curious about why two methodist ministers would be riding in a gentleman's carriage. About two hundred showed up to hear what these strange men had to say.

The meeting was a success, and news of future meetings spread quickly by word of mouth. Whitefield traveled throughout the area of Bristol, preaching from ladders, roofs, and market spaces. When he returned to the miners in Kingswood on February 21, nearly two thousand people waited to hear him. Within four days the crowds had grown to more than ten thousand. "The fire is kindled in the country; and I know, all the devils in hell shall not be able to quench it," Whitefield exclaimed.[1]

The young preacher discovered quickly how to make effective use of the natural acoustics in the open. He usually spoke from a raised area, whether hill or rooftop, so he could often be heard by tens of thousands of people.

He also experienced more freedom in his speaking. Though he continued to wear the long black gown that identified him as a minister, he was no longer confined to one of the large, raised pulpits that were found in most churches at that time. Since he was no longer forced to stand in one place, Whitefield would often move back and forth in front of his audience as if he were on a stage. In the places where he was now preaching, there was no need to conduct a complete Anglican worship service, so his sermon became the focus of everyone's attention.

And these sermons were now well-rehearsed dramatic presentations, given without notes. Whitefield had begun to preach and pray extemporaneously during his first voyage to America. Even the best preachers appeared weak and passionless when compared to Whitefield. They were at a disadvantage as long as they read their sermons in a "dignified" manner from carefully prepared notes and remained behind their dark wooden pulpits.

Whitefield's style of speaking wasn't without its dangers. It "often occasioned many inward conflicts," he confided to his friend and biographer John Gillies. "Sometimes, when twenty thousand people were before me, I had not, in my apprehension, a word to say either to God or them." He responded to his fears by praying intensely, often right up to the moment when he had to begin speaking. "I was never totally deserted," he reported.[2]

In March Whitefield and Howell Harris met at Cardiff, Wales, where they preached together. Whitefield spoke in English and Harris in Welsh. Harris was about as physically intimidating as Whitefield was not, but despite their outward differences, the two friends had many similarities. They were born in the same year, had both attended Oxford, and both experienced strained relationships with the hierarchy of the Church of England. While Whitefield never left the church, Harris did.

Whitefield seemed to enjoy his conflicts with other priests and Church of England bishops. By mid-April he and William Seward were ready to take on London. Their arrival was announced in advance, and they quickly received the expected official refusal to use the churches. "Let not the adversaries say, I have thrust myself out of their synagogues," Whitefield proclaimed. "No, they have thrust me out. And since the self-righteous men of this generation count themselves unworthy, I go out into the highways and hedges, and compel harlots, publicans, and sinners to come in, that my Master's house may be filled."[3] These words were not calculated to smooth ruffled feathers within the church establishment.

As spring became summer, not only were bishops and priests objecting to Whitefield's preaching methods, but parts of the religious press were as well. Chief among those critics was the *Weekly Miscellany,* which represented opinions of the Church of England. It criticized Whitefield for his overly dramatic speaking style and for, in essence, competing with his own church for people.

And Whitefield was nothing if not dramatic. He could move rapidly from rage to fear, or from the utter despair of those without Christ to the religious ecstacy of the new birth. Tears were often his best tool for communication with a wide variety of people.

He loved speaking at the Kensington scaffold, a permanent structure used for hangings. One of his favorite sermons given at that location described the last moment of hardened criminals: "The prisoners tomorrow will have their hands tied behind them, their thumbstrings must be put on, and their fetters knocked off; they must be tied fast to the cart, the cap put over their faces, and the dreadful signal given: if you were their relations would not you weep? Don't be angry then with a poor minister for weeping over them that will not weep for themselves."[4]

The more the establishment criticized Whitefield, the larger the crowds that flocked to see him. By July increasing numbers of carriages were appearing at his meetings, indicating the presence of the upper classes.

George Whitefield's success with "field meetings," as they came to be called, convinced John and Charles Wesley that they should adapt this approach to their ministry. In fact, Whitefield persuaded John Wesley to take over the meetings in the Bristol area.

But all was not well in the friendship between Whitefield and the two brothers. John Wesley was known for airing his opinions freely and believing that they were always right. Before turning the Bristol meetings over to Wesley, Whitefield asked him to focus on the new birth rather than preaching about points of doctrine. Four weeks into his ministry at Bristol, however, John Wesley gave a sermon in which he renounced the doctrine of predestination, the teaching that from the beginning God chose which individuals would turn to faith in Christ.

Having witnessed strong emotional responses among those who repented during his sermons and having cast lots for guidance (a practice he had learned from the Moravians), Wesley later said that he was convinced that he gave this sermon in direct obedience to God's direction.

Whitefield, working in London, knew nothing of Wesley's sermon or of his plans to have it printed. He personally leaned toward the Calvinist belief in predestination. When weeks later he learned of Wesley's actions, he wrote to his friend, "What will be the consequences but controversy? If people ask my opinion, what shall I do? . . . Silence on both sides will be best. It is noised abroad already that there is a division between you and me, and my heart within me is grieved."

John Wesley refused to budge. He next developed the teaching called Christian perfection. While many Christians equate Christian perfection with Christian maturity, Wesley maintained that on this earth, Christians could attain a state where the sin nature was eradicated. He saw this as a second stage of Christian experience in which a Christian received by faith the gift of being perfect.

Between his teachings on predestination and Christian perfection, John Wesley was laying the foundations for a unique faction of methodism with himself as the leader. George Whitefield was genuinely distressed at actions on his friend's part which would inevitably cause division among the people they were bringing to Christ. For the time being, however, he maintained his silence, hoping and praying that John Wesley might change his mind. He also began making plans to travel with William Seward and another friend to America so that he could deliver the funds he had raised for the orphanage and preach throughout the colonies.

News of Whitefield's huge meetings in both Bristol and London had reached America. During the previous decade, the northern colonies in particular had been experiencing revival under the ministry of Jonathan Edwards and other preachers. Controversy erupted, with camps dividing themselves between the New Light (the equivalent of England's "new birth" advocates) and the Old Light. When word arrived that George White-field was planning on traveling to the American colonies, intending to preach wherever he had the opportunity, New Light followers were filled with anticipation.

George Whitefield and his two friends landed at Lewes, Delaware, on October 30, 1739. In response to a request by the town's mayor, the next day Whitefield preached a sermon, and then he and his party started on the roughly 150-mile journey to Philadelphia. Riding horseback, the three men completed the trip in three days.

Whitefield chose Philadelphia as his first stop for several reasons. It was centrally located in the colonies, which stretched along more than thirteen hundred miles of coastline. This made it a perfect base of operations. An important port and center of information, Philadel-phia was a logical place for Whitefield to learn the best places to procure materials for building the orphanage in Georgia.

At first, Philadelphia lived up to its name as "the city of brotherly love" in how it received Whitefield. He was welcomed warmly by pastors of the various churches as well as by the laypeople. Pulpits were open to him, but by the first Thursday after his arrival, he'd been asked to preach somewhere other than a church and held his first outdoor meeting. He preached on the courthouse stairs to about six thousand people.

Some of the interest was the result of William Seward's hard work. Every day, Seward wrote as many as one hundred letters to people in the area, informing them of Whitefield's presence and his speaking plans. When trips were planned to smaller neighboring settlements or to larger cities in nearby colonies, Seward again wrote to people in advance so that larger crowds would be prepared to hear the evangelist.

But just as he had done in England, Whitefield soon managed to stir up problems with the local clergy. When he learned that a New Light presbyterian preacher, the Reverend William Tennent, was battling the perceived deadness and formality of the churches, Whitefield immediately entered the fray.

He recorded in his journals the approach he took to the issue during a Sunday afternoon meeting: "I was much carried out in bearing my testimony against the unchristian principles and practices of our clergy. Three of my reverend brethren were present; I know not whether they were offended. I endeavored to speak with meekness as well as zeal. . . . If I want to convince Church of England Protestants, I must prove that the generality of their teachers do not preach or live up to the truth as it is in Jesus. In vain do we hope to set people right till we demonstrate that the way which they have been taught is wrong."

Finding themselves the target of Whitefield's public attacks, Church of England ministers in America closed their pulpits to him. That suited Whitefield perfectly. He knew from his experiences in England that criticism from the church hierarchy almost always led to larger crowds at his meetings. And he wanted to be perceived as a minister of Jesus Christ, not a minister of the denomination to which he was officially tied.

After nine days in Philadelphia, Whitefield left for New York to visit Thomas Noble, a wealthy man who had written Whitefield, indicating an interest in supporting the Georgia orphanage.

While there, he asked a Mr. Vessey for permission to preach in Anglican churches. Whitefield wrote in his journals that "he charged me with making a disturbance in Philadelphia, and sowing and causing division in other places." Again, Whitefield was not concerned with tact. After accusing Mr. Vessey of going against the canons of the church by visiting public houses, or taverns, Whitefield went on to tell him that "if they preached the gospel, I wished them good luck in the name of the Lord." To suggest to a fellow minister much older than himself that he might not be preaching the gospel was a terrible insult. Not surprisingly, Mr. Vessey denied Whitefield permission to preach in the churches, so the young itinerant once again preached in the fields.

Whitefield seemed completely unconcerned about the real pain and controversy he was causing. He spoke two or more times a day and then returned to Philadelphia. With winter weather threatening, he and his traveling companions headed toward Georgia, where he planned on starting the construction of the orphanage. Once he arrived, however, other issues caught up with him.

five

Shortly before George Whitefield left England in 1739, he met a Christian young woman named Elizabeth Delamotte. Her father was quite wealthy and operated a sugar importing business. Whitefield had studiously avoided developing friendships with women, but Elizabeth appealed to him in a way no other woman ever had.

Whitefield felt that he could not love God completely if he also loved a woman. His understanding of holiness demanded that all passions, of whatever kind, be directed only toward God. There was no room in his theology for romantic love.

When he first arrived in the colonies, Whitefield immersed himself in his work, in part to push thoughts of Elizabeth from his mind. But once he arrived in Savannah, Georgia, in early January 1740, he found a letter from Elizabeth waiting for him. This communication renewed his internal struggles about his feelings toward her.

Meanwhile, plenty of other matters were crying for his attention. The day after his arrival in Savannah, he went with James Habersham to visit a tract of land, about ten miles away, that Habersham had chosen as the site for the future orphanage. The five-hundred-acre parcel was partially cleared, and cows and poultry were already being kept there. Much work still had to be done—primarily the construction of the orphanage buildings—before any orphans could make use of it. "I called it Bethesda, that is, The House of Mercy," Whitefield said, "for I hope many acts of mercy will be shown there."

Whitefield returned to Savannah, excited about the future prospects of the orphanage, but also concerned about the immediate welfare of the orphans. He rented the largest house available and soon had more than twenty orphans living in it. He also placed a Dr. Hunter in charge of an infirmary for the children and stocked it with medicine he had brought with him from England.

During the three months Whitefield spent traveling through the colonies on his way to Georgia, he had had many opportunities to observe slavery in action. Within two weeks of his arrival in Savannah, he wrote an open letter addressed "to the Inhabitants of Maryland, Virginia, and North and South Carolina." In it, he expressed his views on slavery:

> *Whether it be lawful for Christians to buy*
> *slaves, I shall not take upon me to determine;*
> *but sure I am it is sinful, when bought, to use*

*them worse than brutes; and, I fear, the general-
ity of you, who own [slaves], are liable to such
a charge; for your slaves, I believe, work as
hard as the horses whereon you ride.*

*These, after they have done their work, are
fed and taken proper care of; but many [slaves],
when wearied with labour in your plantations,
have been obliged to grind their own corn after
they return home.*

*Your dogs are caressed and fondled at your
tables; but your slaves, who are frequently
styled dogs or beasts, have not an equal privi-
lege. They are scarce permitted to pick up the
crumbs which fall from their masters' tables.
Nay, some, as I have been informed by an eye-
witness, have been, upon the most trifling
provocation, cut with knives, and have had forks
thrown into their flesh: not to mention what
numbers have been given up to the inhuman
usage of cruel taskmasters, who, by their unrelenting scourges, have ploughed upon their
backs, and made long furrows, and, at length,
brought them even to death itself. . . .*

*Is it not the highest ingratitude, as well as
cruelty, not to let your poor slaves enjoy some
fruits of their labour? Whilst I have viewed your
plantations cleared and cultivated, and have
seen many spacious houses built, and the owners of them faring sumptuously every day, my
blood has almost run cold within me, when
I have considered how many of your slaves
had neither convenient food to eat, nor proper*

raiment to put on, notwithstanding most of the
comforts you enjoy were solely owing to their
indefatigable labours. The Scripture says,
"Thou shalt not muzzle the ox that treadeth out
the corn." Does God take care of oxen? And will
He not take care of [slaves]? Undoubtedly He
will. "Go to now, ye rich men, weep and howl
for your miseries that shall come upon you."
Behold, the provision of the poor [slaves],
which have reaped down your fields, which is by
you denied them, "crieth, and the cries of them
which have reaped are entered into the ears of
the Lord of Sabaoth."

The letter was picked up by newspapers throughout the colonies, including those owned by Benjamin Franklin. They stirred up quite a bit of controversy. Wealthy plantation owners were not accustomed to being publicly denounced.

While today Christians believe it is wrong to own slaves, and George Whitefield is criticized for not completely recognizing the evils of the slave trade, he does deserve credit for what he did for slaves at a time when many white people rejected the fact that black people, too, had souls. To begin with, he used his position as a prominent evangelist to argue for better treatment of slaves, and he developed a biblical basis for his arguments. Second, he insisted on being able to preach to slaves wherever he went and is considered largely responsible for bringing organized Christianity to the slave population. Third, he promoted the cause of educating slaves, giving them both trades and the ability to read and write, at a time when many white people thought such efforts were a waste of resources.

While Whitefield was causing controversy in defending legitimate causes, he was also offending people needlessly. Whether this was intentional or due to immaturity is debated, but it seems clear that he didn't help himself with a February 1740 sermon in which he denounced the clergy as "slothful shepherds and dumb dogs." He also declared that the highly popular archbishop of Canterbury, John Tillotson (who had died before Whitefield was born), had "sent thousands to hell."

As signs of spring moved northward through the colonies, Whitefield prepared to leave the orphans and the construction of the orphanage under James Habersham's supervision once again and make a preaching tour of the American colonies. But before he left Georgia in April, he decided to stop wrestling with his feelings for Elizabeth Delamotte and instead take action. He wrote two letters, one to her and one to her parents.

In the letter to her parents, he asked for their daughter's hand in marriage. "You need not be afraid of sending me a refusal," he wrote, "for, I bless God, if I know anything of my own heart, I am free from that foolish passion, which the world calls *love*. I write, only because I believe it is the will of God that I should alter my state; but your denial will fully convince me, that your daughter is not the person appointed by God for me."

While that letter was hardly designed to reassure two loving parents about the wisdom of letting their daughter marry a man who would take her thousands of miles from England, Whitefield's letter to Elizabeth was almost calculated to earn her refusal. He spoke no words of love. Instead he asked, "Do you think you could undergo the fatigues that must necessarily attend being joined to one who is every day liable to be called to suffer for the sake of Jesus Christ? . . . Can you, when you have a husband, be as though you had none, and willingly part with him, even for a long season, when his Lord and Master shall call him forth to preach the gospel, and command him to leave you behind?"

Later in the letter he explained, "I make no great profession to you, because I believe you think me sincere. The passionate expressions which carnal courtiers use, I think, ought to be avoided by those that would marry in the Lord. I can only promise, by the help of God, to keep my matrimonial vow, and to do what I can towards helping you forward in the great work of your salvation."

The letters having been sent on their way to England and the matter from Whitefield's perspective taken out of his hands, he then prepared to head once again to Philadelphia with William Seward. Conflict between the New Lights and the Old Lights had reached fever pitch in that city since Whitefield had left it for Georgia four months before. Benjamin Franklin only added fuel to the fire by reprinting Whitefield's comments that questioned the faith of the late Archbishop of Canterbury John Tillotson.

Under the circumstances, it is hardly surprising that Whitefield was refused the use of Church of England pulpits in Philadelphia when he arrived on April 14. But his friends built a stage on a hill, and crowds varying in number from five thousand to fifteen thousand crowded around to hear him. Many people, both black and white, came to see him after meetings to ask for his advice and prayers. Commenting on the unavailability of the churches, Whitefield noted, "Little do my enemies think what service they do me. If they did, one would think, out of spite they would even desist from opposing me."[1]

Because Whitefield had already preached in Phila-delphia and felt that he was well-known in the city, he asked for funds to support the Georgia orphanage. This approach became his standard practice. He never asked for money in an area until he had already visited it because he did not want orphanage fund-raising to take precedence over preaching the gospel.

He spent nine days in Philadelphia, and during that time Whitefield came up with the idea of building a school for blacks in the area. His wealthy friend William Seward advanced money to secure five thousand acres for the purpose and left for England to secure further support for the project. Unfortunately, the plans collapsed a few months later when Seward was killed while preaching in Wales.

Other projects had more success. After Whitefield left Philadelphia, outdoor meetings continued. Accord-ing to Benjamin Franklin, people perceived the need for some permanent structure where preachers of any religious persuasion would be able to speak. These community-minded individuals raised money for both land and a building and planned for it to be a church on Sundays and a charity school during the week. On his return trip, Whitefield spoke in the new building. It was used primarily by William Tennent and his son, but eventually the congregation connected with it moved to a different building, and the charity school ultimately evolved into the University of Pennsylvania.

Whitefield reported to the orphanage after his trip to Philadelphia. Here he met with an incensed board of trustees, who were all faithful members of the Church of England. Having read many reports of Whitefield's attacks on the church, these men feared Whitefield would try to turn the orphanage into an independent methodist organization. They insisted that Whitefield submit to their authority, they denied him any right to deed the orphanage to another party in his will, and they demanded that he present them with a full accounting of the finances.

George Whitefield may have been only twenty-five years old, but he thoroughly understood the power of the press. Faced with this situation, he immediately gave his side of the story to various colonial newspapers. He would submit his financial accountings to the public who had entrusted him with the funds, not to a group of trustees who, in his view, had done little to advance the cause of the orphans.

Thoroughly put out, Commissary Alexander Garden denied Whitefield access to any Church of England pulpits in the area and charged him in the church court with "railing Accusation against the clergy of the *Church of England* in general, and the present *Bishop of London* in particular."[2]

Most colonists did not hold any special ties to the Church of England and cared even less about the bishop of London. Due to Whitefield's skillful use of the press, they perceived Whitefield as a persecuted underdog who cared about the well-being of the poor and oppressed more than the sensibilities of the rich and powerful. Once again, opposition from the church establishment increased Whitefield's popularity, and church officials realized too late how they were playing into his hands.

The end result of this conflict was that Whitefield preached to ever larger crowds; the New England colonies where he intended to speak in the fall were eager to hear from this firebrand. Also, he remained the de facto head of the orphanage. Privately, however, he was concerned enough about the actions of Commissary Garden and the church court that he sent a letter directly to the bishop of London, asking for his opinion as to whether Garden had the authority to convene the church court.

Though by this time Whitefield clearly believed in salvation by faith alone, the remnants of his pre-conversion emphasis on intense religious activity as the only path to holiness still clung to him. There seemed to remain within him a sense of unworthiness before God. This seed of self-doubt caused Whitefield to push himself relentlessly, as if God were just waiting to strike out at him if he decreased his religious exertions even a little.

So it is not surprising that during the summer of 1740 Whitefield began having more frequent problems with his health. He also firmly established a pattern of ignoring his illnesses as much as possible and persisting in preaching at least once a day no matter what. In September he took a ship north to Rhode Island, and from there traveled to Boston.

New England had been the birthplace of the New Light Revival, which is now often called the Great

Awakening, during the 1730s. One of the major participants in this revival was Jonathan Edwards, a preacher from Northampton, Massachusetts, who wrote an account of the revivals called *A Narrative of Surprising Conversions*. It quickly became a best-seller in America, England, and Scotland. George Whitefield acquired a copy while he was in Philadelphia months before he arrived in Boston in the fall of 1740.

As it had throughout this second trip to the colonies, publicity worked to Whitefield's advantage. Only one newspaper, run by Thomas Fleet, opposed the evangelist, and its negative articles simply aroused even more curiosity among the public. Crowds numbering in the tens of thousands flocked to hear the man preach. Often, more people were in the crowds than lived in the towns where the meetings were held.

Inevitably, the size of the crowds led to tragedy. A meetinghouse in Boston was filled beyond its capacity before Whitefield cver arrived. Someone in the gallery broke a board to make a seat. The sound sent panic through the crowd. People rushed to escape. Children and women were thrown from the windows, fell to the ground, and were trampled. Before order was restored, five people had been killed.

To everyone's surprise, Whitefield insisted on preaching and simply moved the location of his meeting to the common. He spoke to the crowd through a driving rainstorm. No one left.

Tragic as the incident was, it did offer lessons in crowd control. From that point on, Whitefield was much more careful about maintaining order in buildings where he preached, although on one occasion he had to climb through a window in order to reach the pulpit.

As long as Whitefield's sermons stuck to the new birth, he was widely praised. He had developed a habit of taking on the clergy, however, and it wasn't long before he was suggesting that some of the New England ministers were dead to the gospel themselves. These attacks, along with public statements questioning the quality of education ministers received at Harvard and Yale, aroused great anger among many members of the establishment.

Whitefield also planted seeds of discontent among the younger members of the clergy toward their elders and between the general public and their pastors. The serious problems this would cause weren't recognized immediately. Instead, Whitefield continued to travel throughout New England to generally great acclaim. He raised large amounts of money for the orphanage, and in October he had a long-awaited meeting in Northampton, Massachusetts, with Jonathan Edwards. Because of differences in personality and in how they approached theology, the two men never became close friends. But they did admire and respect each other greatly.

On October 9 George Whitefield preached a farewell sermon in Boston and prepared to head back to Georgia. Seeing many clergy in the audience, he chose the story of Nicodemus going to Jesus by night and created yet another opportunity to charge members of the clergy with not knowing the Lord whom they professed to serve. Because of such incidents, many preachers in New England who supported Whitefield when he first arrived expressed reservations about him as he left.

Whitefield returned to Georgia, taking advantage of every opportunity to preach along the way. Near the end of November, he received several months' worth of correspondence from England that had arrived by ship. Included in the letters were two devastating pieces of news. First, Elizabeth Delamotte wrote to decline his offer of marriage. Second, he received word of the death of his friend William Seward.

Seward's death was not only the personal loss of a close friend—it also was the loss of a major financial contributor to the orphanage. For most of the rest of his life, the monetary needs of the orphanage would weigh heavily on Whitefield's mind, and much of his energy would be devoted to providing for the orphans whom he viewed as part of an extended family.

Other letters in the correspondence made clear the deepening rift with his friend John Wesley. In some ways, Whitefield relished his conflicts with the church establishment. But the disagreement with Wesley was not simply an intellectual exercise or an opportunity for greater publicity. It tore at the fabric of Whitefield's soul and caused him deep pain. On January 16, 1741, George Whitefield left for England, knowing that a direct confrontation with his old friend could not be avoided much longer.

six

During his two-month trip back to England aboard the *Minerva,* George Whitefield had plenty of time to think about the problems that had been developing in his relationship with the Wesley brothers, particularly John. When he had left England a year and a half earlier, Whitefield had recognized the increasing tensions. While Whitefield was leaning toward Calvinist beliefs, including predestination, John publicly denied the doctrine of predestination and developed the doctrine of Christian perfection. At the time, Whitefield had chosen to ignore the matter in hopes that it would solve itself.

By 1741 it was clear that things would not improve. In fact, during Whitefield's absence, the situation had gotten much worse. Some of these changes Whitefield had learned about through letters from the Wesley brothers and from supportive friends in England such as

Howell Harris and William Seward.

To begin with, not long after Whitefield left England in 1739, John Wesley published his sermon against predestination and had it distributed throughout the various groups or societies within the revival movement. He also sent copies to many people in the American colonies, including Commissary Alexander Garden, one of Whitefield's harshest critics.

This action was taken in spite of Whitefield's repeated requests that Wesley not divide the movement by preaching against a doctrine so many people held. As a point of fact, any priest ordained in the Church of England—including the Wesley brothers and Whitefield—was required to agree to the doctrine of predestination. While Wesley's printed sermon did not mention Whitefield by name, it was common knowledge that Whitefield held to the Church of England teaching in this matter. The sermon drew public attention to the fact that Wesley disagreed with Whitefield.

That fall the Wesley brothers printed a new hymn-book. Many of the hymns were written by Charles and focused on commonly held beliefs. But one hymn spoke directly to the issue of predestination and caused almost as great a stir as his brother John's sermon had.

John Wesley also began solidifying the temporary leadership of the movement Whitefield had entrusted to him during Whitefield's absence from England. He claimed ownership of a school building in Kingswood for which Whitefield had raised money and laid the cornerstone. This action in itself upset many Whitefield supporters. Then Wesley moved his headquarters from

Bristol to London, establishing a society in London that met in an old cannon foundry. He began calling his movement the United Society and forcing out any members who did not agree with his positions on predestination and Christian perfection.

During 1740 Wesley broke with the Moravians. While many leaders within methodism did not agree with certain Moravian teachings, contemporary accounts suggest that Wesley went out of his way to create conflict within the Moravians meeting in London. Some of these people were methodists. Some were not. James Hutton, who wrote a history of the Moravians, stated, "John Wesley being resolved to do all things himself. . .is at enmity against the Brethren. Envy is not extinct in him. . . ." Describing the split within the London group, Hutton wrote, "We asked his forgiveness, if in anything we had aggrieved him, but he continued full of wrath, accusing the Brethren that they, by dwelling exclusively on the doctrine of faith, neglected the law and zeal for sanctification. In short, he became our declared opponent, and the two Societies of the Brethren and the Methodists were thenceforth separated."

Hutton was not the only person concerned about Wesley's attitudes during this period. Howell Harris's journals reflect the views of a man caught in the middle of a conflict between good friends, and not knowing whose side to take:

Am in sore distress, Brother Seward having testified against the Wesleys, and I hearing still of their love and power, am in fear lest I do wrong on both sides. O Lord, bless the dear Wesleys!

*O! is not John Wesley thy dear child. Suffer
him not to rail against the truth in ignorance.*

*Heard things that staggered me sore as to
Mr. Wesley, lording over God's heritage. . . . O
Lord, show by some means of John Wesley, what
he is. . . .*

*Spent some time about what to think of Mr.
Wesley. I am in the dark, had heart to wrestle
for him, fearing of all sides lest I err.*

Harris also received a letter complaining about John Wesley's behavior: "By his rash and inconsiderate speeches he has not only grieved ye hearts of God's people, but has given occasion for the enemies of the Lord to rejoice. . . . Such notorious instances of his forgetting himself in ye heat of controversy, that in justice to ye truth. . .ought to be made public."

Aware of all these incidents, Whitefield wrote to the Wesleys from the ship, claiming that their actions would force him to speak publicly about these doctrinal issues, something he had largely avoided to this point.

The London to which George Whitefield returned in March 1741 was not the same city he had left in 1739. Members of the revival were split over whether to follow Whitefield or Wesley. Copies of Whitefield's imprudent attacks on Archbishop Tillotson had caused other supporters to change their opinion of him. And while Whitefield was on the *Minerva* heading toward England, John Wesley did one more thing that caused great controversy among methodists.

On February 28 Wesley removed John Cennick from

the group; Cennick was a young, talented preacher who was loved by the methodist society at Kingswood. Cennick had written to Whitefield, telling him about the dissension that John Wesley was creating and encouraging Whitefield to return to England. Whitefield never got the letter. Somehow, John Wesley got his hands on it.

Based on the letter, he charged Cennick with "scoffing at the Word and ministers of God, tale-bearing, backbiting, evil speaking, dissembling, lying and slandering." He did not give Cennick or his associates the opportunity to present their side of the issue. Instead, according to John Wesley's journals, "I, John Wesley, by the consent and approbation of the band-society in Kingswood, do declare the persons above-mentioned, to be no longer members thereof." Fifty-two people left with Cennick. Close to ninety remained with John Wesley.

One of the first things on Whitefield's agenda was to have a private meeting with John and Charles Wesley in London and see if they could sort out their problems. After Whitefield's previous trip to America, John Wesley had hurried to London to meet with him. This time John did not immediately make the journey from Bristol to the capital. Some people think he was not eager to meet with Whitefield after turning so many supporters against him during his absence. Others simply maintain that various responsibilities kept John Wesley from traveling right away. In any event, Charles Wesley and George Whitefield met, but were unable to bridge their doctrinal differences.

As a result, Whitefield faced a grim situation, which he outlined in a March 25 letter to James Habersham, the manager of the orphanage. Explaining why he was not sending money for the work, he said:

It has been a trying time with me. A large orphan family, consisting of near a hundred, to be maintained, about four thousand miles off, without the least fund, and in the [poorest] part of his Majesty's dominions; also about a thousand pounds in debt for them, and not worth twenty pounds in the world of my own, and threatened to be arrested for three hundred and fifty pounds, drawn for in favour of the Orphan-house, by my late dear deceased friend and fellow-traveller Mr. S[eward].

My Bookseller, who, I believe, has got some hundreds by me, being drawn away by the M[oravia]ns, refuses to print for me; and many, very many of my spiritual children, who, at my last departure from England, would have plucked out their own eyes to have given to me, are so prejudiced by the dear Messrs. W[esley]'s dressing up the doctrine of Election in such horrible colours, that they will neither hear, see, nor give me the least assistance: Yea, some of them send threatening letters, that God will speedily destroy me.

As for the people of the world, they are so imbittered by my injudicious and too severe expressions against Archbishop Tillotson, and the author of The Whole Duty of Man, *that they fly from me as from a viper; and what is most cutting of all, I am now constrained, on account of our differing in principles, publicly to separate*

79

*from my dear, dear old friends, Messrs. J[ohn]
and C[harles] W[esle]y, whom I still love as my
own soul:*

*But, through infinite mercy, I am enabled to
strengthen myself in the Lord my God. I am cast
down but not destroyed, perplexed but not in
despair. . . . I have not, nor can I as yet, make
any collections; but let us not fear. Our heavenly Father, with whom the fatherless find
mercy, will yet provide.*

Whitefield was not exaggerating when he said many
of those he had led to faith in Christ would not listen to
him. Letters from the Wesleys, as well as accounts written by their followers, state that the Wesley brothers
instructed their followers, to plug their ears when they
passed by an area where George Whitefield was preaching so that they wouldn't be corrupted by his words.
They tell of people literally putting their fingers in their
ears and racing by any Whitefield-led gathering.

It is also important to note a painful lesson Whitefield
had apparently learned from his reception in England.
He realized that John Wesley's words against him were
no worse than what Whitefield himself had said about
Archbishop Tillotson, and he recognized that he was
wrong to have attacked the man in the way he had. Only
twenty-six years old, Whitefield had matured enough to
acknowledge that his own words were "injudicious" and
"too severe." In many ways, this was a watershed in
George Whitefield's ministry. From the time he was so
severely attacked by a man he considered to be one of
his best friends, he seemed much less eager to heedlessly

indict others and much more sensitive to how things he did and said might strike other people.

Whitefield was not, however, without friends. A building in the Moorefields section of London was already under construction for Whitefield to use in preaching. At first he expressed concerns that it was too close to Wesley's Foundry and might be considered intentional competition. But his supporters persisted in completing the structure and Whitefield relented, calling it the Tabernacle.

While the Tabernacle was under construction, Whitefield preached in the open. He gave his standard evangelistic messages and also began addressing some of the doctrinal issues that had been creating such confusion and dissension among his followers. At first, crowds numbered only in the low hundreds, a humiliating experience for someone who was used to speaking to more than ten thousand at a time. But gradually the size of the crowds increased.

He also met with John Cennick and took the young man on as an assistant. They agreed to write for a weekly paper published by John Lewis in London. Called *The Weekly History,* the paper recorded news of revival activities in both Britain and America.

These activities were in full swing when, at the end of March, John Wesley came to visit. It was the first time the two men had seen each other since Whitefield had asked Wesley to look after his followers while he traveled to America. As in the conversation with Charles, Whitefield could not reconcile his position with that of John.

At this point, Whitefield had his response to John

Wesley's sermon on predestination printed and distributed. In it, Whitefield dealt with the issue of whether casting lots was a reliable way to determine God's leading. He felt it essential to deal with this issue because Wesley had cast lots as part of the process of deciding that he should speak out against predestination, and then in his printed sermon had used that fact as part of the validation of his arguments. When Whitefield took up the subject of lots, he mentioned a time when Wesley had cast lots and they had been in error. Wesley saw this as a terrible betrayal on Whitefield's part. He once again visited Whitefield, told him what he found objectionable about his printed response, and said that Whitefield had caused "an open (and probably irreparable) breach" between them.

On that unyielding note, the two men parted company. The Wesley brothers perceived Whitefield as a dangerous man. They published sermons, hymns, and pamphlets that took direct issue with Whitefield's teachings. They followed Whitefield wherever he preached, giving "corrective" sermons after he left.

After Whitefield went to Kingswood, he wrote a letter to John Wesley, asking him about various reports he had heard about both Wesley's claim to the school building and his treatment of John Cennick. Wesley replied in a letter that, among other things, criticized Whitefield's treatment of him. "A Spaniard would have behaved more tenderly to his English prisoners," Wesley wrote. Near the end of the letter, he wondered what would happen if he were to treat Whitefield in the same way as he believed Whitefield was treating him. "But you are very safe," he wrote. "I cannot meet you here. This field you have all to yourself. I cannot dwell on those things, which have an immediate tendency to make you odious and contemptible. The general tenor both of my public and private exhortations, when I touch thereon at all (as even my enemies know if they would testify), is 'Spare the young man, even Absalom, for my sake.' "

It is ironic that John Wesley would compare himself to King David and Whitefield to David's treacherous son Absalom, given that Whitefield had come to faith long before Wesley, had done the original building of methodist societies, and had encouraged Wesley to adopt his method of field preaching.

John Wesley's letter apparently affected George Whitefield greatly. Howell Harris visited Whitefield at that time. "Sick and vomiting, he wept with strong cryings and weeping," Harris reported, and he "poured out his soul before the Lord." Whitefield biographer Arnold Dallimore cites four changes to Whitefield's ministry after he received John Wesley's letter:

1. He took no further action in the matter of the Kingswood property.
2. He remained publicly silent about the actual conflict with the Wesleys. This decision may have contributed to Whitefield no longer publishing his daily journals.
3. He stopped pointing out the imperfections of those people who professed to have attained perfection.
4. Although he continued to stand for what he believed to be God's eternal truths, he became even more careful to avoid saying or printing anything with which Wesley could find fault.

In June 1741 Whitefield wrote, "The heat of the battle is now, I hope, pretty well over. God is pleased to give me great power, and to strengthen me both in body and soul. Our congregations are large. . . . A wonderful power attends the word preached."

While the broken pieces of George Whitefield's ministry in England had been repaired and arguably made stronger from the mending, the rift between Whitefield and the Wesleys would not be bridged for a long time.

seven

Having done everything he could to resolve his dispute with the Wesleys, George Whitefield was ready to leave London. Near the end of June 1741, the twenty-six-year-old evangelist traveled to English towns such as Essex and Suffolk. He held meetings twice a day and raised funds for Bethesda. After the conflict he had just experienced, he was becoming more convinced that he should stay away from denominational ties and focus on evangelism.

"I have no freedom, but in *going about to all denominations,*" he wrote in a letter dated July 13. "I cannot join with any one, so as to be fixed in any particular place. Every one has his proper gift. Field-preaching is my place. In this, I am carried as on eagles' wings. God makes way for me everywhere." That goal was about to be tested. A week and a half later, he left on a six-day journey by ship to Scotland. He had been invited to speak there by the

Erskine brothers, who were members of a group called the Secession Church. They had broken off from the Church of Scotland. Other reformers who remained within the national church also asked him to speak, and Whitefield agreed to speak for them after he had fulfilled his commitment to the Erskines.

Shortly after his arrival in Scotland, Whitefield attended a private meeting of leaders within the Secession Church. The secessionists started teaching Whitefield about their doctrines and why they had separated from the Church of Scotland. "I replied," Whitefield wrote three days later, "they might save themselves that trouble, for I had no scruples about it." He went on to explain that he was focusing on presenting the gospel to everyone.

They told him that they wanted him to preach only within their churches until he better understood the issues they were dealing with. "I asked, why only for them?" Whitefield reported. "Mr. Ralph Erskines said, 'they were the Lord's people.' I then asked, whether there were no other Lord's people but themselves; and, supposing all others were the devil's people, they certainly had more need to be preached to; and, therefore, I was more and more determined to go out into the highways and hedges."

The meeting soon broke up. Whitefield refused to be tied exclusively to the Secession Church, and they responded by preaching publicly against him. Whitefield ignored the attacks and instead continued preaching throughout Scotland for the next three months. He drew huge crowds and became very popular. "I find it best simply to preach the pure gospel, and not to meddle at all with controversy," he wrote to a pastor in Aberdeen.

"The present divisions are a sore judgment to Scotland. This is my comfort, Jesus is king."

He was also cheered by good news from Georgia. Ideal weather and hard work had produced an excellent crop and healthy herds of cattle. Orphanage leaders had finished all the building construction, and aside from the need to pay off its bills, the orphanage was in good shape. Whitefield's efforts on that score were gradually reducing the orphanage's indebtedness, although his critics in Scotland accused him of pocketing the money he collected rather than using it for the orphans.

By the beginning of November, George Whitefield was ready to leave Scotland for Wales. There he fully intended to marry a widow named Elizabeth James, who was about ten years older than he. Whitefield had met Mrs. James on at least two previous occasions during his time in Scotland. He got to know her through his good friend Howell Harris. And it was Howell Harris who had suggested the two get married, in spite of the fact that Harris himself was deeply in love with Mrs. James—a feeling she returned.

Harris first grew aware of his feelings toward Elizabeth James two years earlier, in 1739. She was a sensible woman with no great beauty or fortune. But everyone who met her was struck by her commitment to her faith and her willingness to face hostile crowds while doing the Lord's work. John Wesley called her "a woman of candour and humanity," and Harris frequently spoke of her kindness and tenderness.

Howell Harris and Elizabeth James spoke of marriage, but he never made a definite proposal. Why did he hold back? Like many reformers of his day, he had the unbiblical view that loving a woman would create an obstacle between himself and God. Rather than seeing love as a gift from God that originated at creation, Howell wanted to recreate his feelings immediately after his conversion when "there was no creature between my soul and God." Simply put, Howell Harris saw Elizabeth James as a problem to be solved rather than as a gift to be treasured.

It was at this time that George Whitefield was praying for a woman who could manage the orphan house and be a suitable wife. When Harris heard of this, he immediately realized that this circumstance could solve his predicament. By "resigning her" to his friend Whitefield, as Harris put it, he could help both of them. Elizabeth James would have the security of marriage to a prominent young man, and George Whitefield would have a woman admirably suited to meet his needs. Harris wrote in his journal, "Lord save me from all women and let me have no wife but Thee forever."

After Whitefield returned from America, he and Harris had a conversation about the Welsh widow. Harris then wrote to Mrs. James, suggesting that George Whitefield replace him as a suitor. Convinced that Harris had no intention of marrying Elizabeth James, Whitefield began writing to her about marriage.

Mrs. James was indignant. "If you were my own father you had no right of disposing me against my will," she wrote Howell Harris. She also expressed misgivings about her own ability to work with either of the two preachers. "Oh my friend," she wrote, "beg ye Lord may direct you and your friend to those that are more fit and better qualified for so great a station. . . . 'Tis too great a weight for me to stand under."

She also corresponded with Whitefield, and the more he learned of her through her letters, the more convinced he became that she was the right woman for him. His meetings with her while he was in Scotland did nothing to change his opinion. But she was not so certain. She still had feelings for Howell Harris.

From Elizabeth James's perspective, Howell Harris was attractive for many reasons. They had grown up in the same area of Wales and came from similar backgrounds. They were interested in many of the same things. While Harris had a hard time reaching decisions, she balanced him by being able to make such choices clear. Besides, she had loved him for two years.

Life with George Whitefield, on the other hand, would involve a union of contrasts. She had experienced only small-town life in Wales. Whitefield had already traveled on two continents, speaking to tens of thousands of people. She had an above average education for a woman of her position, but it did not come close to the depth of learning Whitefield had been exposed to. While she could barely read and write, he had earned a degree from Oxford. Whitefield seemed to move easily among the nobility. Elizabeth James found such encounters painfully difficult. And she did not love the man. The one possible attraction that marriage to Whitefield held was the challenge of helping such a man in a complicated ministry.

Apparently, Mrs. James, George Whitefield, and Howell Harris had a meeting when Whitefield arrived in Wales. Harris recorded the event in his diary. He stated that George Whitefield was "full of tenderness and love and simplicity, taking her as from God (having nothing carnal of nature in him), that he feels in his heart solid, rooted and grounded love for her."

Harris also faithfully recorded Elizabeth James's response. "She objected much, about her regards to me & that she could not help it still, & he said he would not love her the less or be jealous. . .and was for marrying now immediately."

Four days later Mrs. James had reached her decision. Perhaps accepting the fact that Howell Harris would never ask her to marry him, no matter how much he really loved her, she agreed to marry George Whitefield. The marriage took place on November 14, 1741, and Howell Harris gave away the bride.

A week later Harris wrote, "Many suspect I was glad to be rid of [Mrs. James] yet the Lord knows what a Burden I felt on parting with so dear a Friend & he knows how gladly I would have married her, even to the last & with what a heart-breaking I gave her up, though with a Resigned Will, & what a loss I saw I had of one that watched over me in the Lord indeed & never was short to me in Faithfulness and Tenderness and Love. . . . I did not feel that love I formerly had felt—not knowing the Reason which now appears. God had intended her for another to make her more happy than she would likely be with me."

George Whitefield himself had a much more pragmatic view of his marriage. He wrote to a friend, "I married. . . one who was a widow, of about thirty-six years of age, and has been a housekeeper for many years; neither rich in fortune nor beautiful as to her person, but, I believe, a true child of God, and one who would not, I think, attempt to hinder me in his work for the world. In that respect, I am just the same as before marriage. I hope God will never suffer me to say, 'I have married a wife, and therefore I cannot come.' "

He certainly made no changes in his lifestyle because of his marriage. The new couple did not take a honeymoon trip. Instead, Whitefield continued preaching twice a day and, in less than a week, left his wife at her home in Wales while he went on a preaching tour throughout England. He returned home to spend Christmas Day with his new wife, but the next day left again for London.

When they married, Whitefield did not have a permanent place to stay. He needed to be more centrally located than in Elizabeth's small cottage in Wales. So three months after they married, he secured an apartment in London, and the small-town Welsh woman moved to the capital city of Great Britain.

While her husband made few changes to his life when he married, Elizabeth Whitefield's life was transformed. She left everyone she had ever known to live in a strange city with different customs and fashions. People judged her as the wife of a famous preacher and were as willing to point out any of her shortcomings as they were those of her husband. She accompanied her husband on two preaching tours, but after that remained home whenever he traveled. Touring the countryside was much more physically demanding in those days than it is today, and she did not have the physical strength to spend months living on the road. Instead, like most women of her day whose husbands traveled for business, she spent months—and sometimes years—living alone in her apartments in London.

The Whitefields' marriage did not match what we understand the ideals of a Christian marriage to be today. While they respected each other, they certainly did not feel romantic love for each other. But they did help each other in their work and came to an understanding of what to expect from each other. Many marriages of their day were much worse.

The first trip which Elizabeth Whitefield took with her husband was to Scotland. They left by ship on May 26, 1742. Ever since Whitefield's first trip to Scotland the previous year, he had been inundated with letters asking him to return. Two small villages outside Glasgow were experiencing revival. One was Cambuslang, and the other was Kilsyth. When the Whitefields arrived in Cambuslang in the middle of July, crowds of more than twenty thousand people turned out to hear the evangelist preach.

The revivals and Whitefield were not without their critics, and Elizabeth Whitefield soon learned how brutal those critics could be. The Erskine brothers and their followers proclaimed a public fast because they viewed the revivals as the work of Satan and George Whitefield as a man set on destroying God's work. In August a thirty-two-page pamphlet attacked Whitefield as "a wandering star, who steers his course according to the compass of gain and advantage." It also described him as "a base English imposter, whom the enemies of Christ's kingdom have chosen as their commander-in-chief, to lead the covenanted kingdom of Scotland back to Egypt and Babylon." Similar writings followed Whitefield throughout his time in Scotland.

In keeping with his standard practice, Whitefield did not publicly respond to his attackers, although in a letter he wrote, "The dear Messrs. Erskines have dressed me in very black colours. . . . Dear men, I pity them. Writing I fear will be in vain. Surely they must grieve the Holy Spirit much."

At the same time, Whitefield learned that the Spanish had invaded Georgia. The orphanage was threatened, so the manager took everyone to a friend's plantation in South Carolina. Six weeks later the Spanish were driven back to Florida and the orphans returned to Bethesda, but many of the residents were sick. Mr. Habersham pleaded with Whitefield to return to Georgia as quickly as possible.

There were signs of good news as well, however. Since the Wesleys and Whitefield had parted ways, Whitefield had begun writing to John Wesley every couple months or so. In early 1742 Whitefield finally received a reply to one of those letters, and while in Scotland he actually met with John Wesley for about an hour. The differences between the two men were not healed, but the relationship began to improve slightly.

In November Whitefield left Scotland for London. He immediately picked up his work at the Tabernacle, which included organizing the services and activities of the congregation as well as preaching to huge crowds. The Countess of Huntingdon and her family were often at Whitefield's services, and their presence drew other members of the British aristocracy as well.

But Whitefield's duties at the Tabernacle had expanded. By 1743 thirty-six religious societies associated with George Whitefield's work were scattered throughout England, and other societies were forming in Scotland and Wales. Itinerant preachers such as Howell Harris worked with these groups, but the societies identified themselves with Whitefield. He was responsible for overseeing how they ran.

Most of the next year and a half was taken up with this work—including addressing the problem of mobs that were attacking the preachers as they did their work. Even in London Whitefield had been shot at while preaching. Other men working for him had been beaten. Mobs had entered meeting houses and kicked and punched the men and torn the clothes from the women.

Finally an incident occurred that sealed Whitefield's determination to take legal action against these rioters. He traveled to Hampton after learning that a mob had seriously injured Thomas Adams, the pastor of the religious society meeting in that town. Once again, a mob attacked. One young woman had her arm broken in two places. Pastor Adams received a deep cut in his leg and was thrown into the pond. Several other people were seriously injured. And when Whitefield appealed to a minister who was also Justice of the Peace, he was told that the mob's behavior was Whitefield's fault because of his preaching.

Before Whitefield took the case to court, he asked all his preachers to meet with him in London and pray and consult with each other. He also wrote to all of his societies, asking them to pray about the situation. Then he took the case to court. The jury found all the defendants guilty. Whitefield had the right to get damages from the defendants, but instead he dropped the matter. He simply wanted to establish a precedent that mobs could not attack religious societies with impunity.

The Whitefields were excited about the verdict, but they also were looking forward to the birth of their first child. Elizabeth Whitefield gave birth to a boy, whom they named John, on October 5. In early 1744 they realized that they could not afford to keep their rented apartment in London and agreed to have Elizabeth and the baby, along with a woman companion, travel to Elizabeth's cottage in Wales. George Whitefield continued with his preaching.

Elizabeth's trip went well until she arrived at the Bell Inn, which was run by Whitefield's brother Richard. The baby became sick and a doctor was called. Despite his best efforts, the baby died. When Whitefield arrived soon afterwards, many encouraged him to stop preaching until the baby was buried. "But I remembered a saying of good Mr. [Matthew] Henry, 'that weeping must not hinder sowing,' " Whitefield later wrote, "and therefore preached twice the next day, and also the day following; on the evening of which, just as I was closing my sermon, the bell struck out for the funeral."

Elizabeth asked her husband to stay with her for a while as they both grieved the loss of their child, but he believed he could not put his work aside. So instead she traveled on to Wales to live in her cottage. When she arrived, she discovered that her husband had sold much of her furniture so that he could give more money to the poor of her village. Her one consolation was that at last she was able to spend time with the people she had known since childhood.

By the summer of that year, disturbing news arrived from

America. Some people who claimed to be Whitefield's followers were involved in religious extremism that discredited his previous work. He soon realized that he had unintentionally set the stage for this problem.

During his previous trip to America, Whitefield had criticized those among the clergy whom he identified as unconverted. He held them responsible for the spiritual lethargy that gripped many churches. He had also referred to impressions made on his mind while reading the Bible. Some people thought he was suggesting that a new period of prophetic ministry had begun that included new revelations from God.

Untrained "exhorters" had begun denouncing anyone who would not submit to their authority as God's newly appointed spokesmen. Some of them were mentally unstable, but they still caused painful divisions within churches and families.

Much of the blame for this development was placed on Whitefield. He felt an obligation to return to America and repair the damage he had unintentionally caused. In August he and Elizabeth Whitefield arrived in Portsmouth, England, ready to set out on a new mission.

eight

In Portsmouth the Whitefields' plans changed when the captain of their scheduled ship refused to receive them as passengers. The captain feared that George Whitefield's preaching would "ruin" his crew.

So the couple left for Plymouth where another ship was scheduled to depart. They were delayed again because war had broken out with France and the ship was ordered to wait for a naval convoy before leaving the safety of the port.

During the six weeks they waited, George immersed himself in preaching, and he established two new societies. He was also nearly murdered. Shortly after the Whitefields arrived in Plymouth, a ship's officer stopped by their lodgings, asking to speak with George Whitefield. The conversation began well enough, but abruptly things changed. "He suddenly rose up," Whitefield wrote, "uttering the most abusive language, calling me *dog, rogue, villain, & c,* and beat me most unmercifully with his gold-headed cane. . . . But my hostess and her daughter hearing me cry *murder,* rushed into the room and seized him by the collar; however, he immediately disengaged himself from them, and repeated his blows upon me."

A second attacker appeared, and the assault ended only after the noise drew the attention of people in neighboring homes.

In August the convoy arrived, and the Whitefields began their crossing of the Atlantic. The crossing was extremely rough and took longer than usual. Storms battered the ship. By the time Whitefield reached land on October 26, 1744, the twenty-nine-year-old preacher was in precarious health. He refused to let this stop him from beginning to preach in the area around what is now York, Maine. He hoped that the excitement he always felt in front of a crowd would ease his physical sufferings.

It did not work. Within a week he collapsed. He had a high fever and his body shook with pain. Two doctors were called in to treat him. Many people thought Whitefield would die at any moment. They prayed day and night for his recovery.

For unknown reasons, someone announced that Whitefield would be preaching and gave a time and place for the meeting. When Whitefield learned that so many ministers and laypeople were gathering to hear him speak, he insisted on getting out of his sick bed and preaching. "Whilst the doctor was preparing a medicine," he wrote, "I on a sudden cried, 'Doctor, my pains are suspended; by the help of God I will go and preach and then come home and die.' "

Fully expecting to die, Whitefield preached with unusual fervency. "Such effects followed the word, that I thought it worth dying for a thousand times," he said. When he returned to the home where he and his wife were staying, he was very sick. They placed him in a bed right by the fire, and he heard friends announce that he was gone.

But slowly Whitefield recovered, although never completely. At one point, as Whitefield still lay by the fire, an African-American woman came in and sat next to him. She stared into his eyes and said, "Master, you must have gotten to Heaven's gate. But Jesus Christ said, Get you down, get you down, you must not come here yet; but go first and call some more poor [black people]." Whitefield was moved by the woman's words and prayed that he would be able to have such a ministry.

His immediate job, however, was to deal with the problems that had erupted since his last visit. Although still weak, he traveled to Boston. When he met with his supporters in that city, he quickly discovered that even they had questions about his teachings.

Since Whitefield had left that city four years earlier, the work of a Reverend James Davenport had created huge divisions within churches of every denomination. Actually, Mr. Davenport was mentally ill and later apologized for his behavior, but at the time he held great influence. Citing comments Whitefield had made while in the colonies, Davenport went around proclaiming which pastors were "converted" and which were not. He demanded that his followers burn possessions and break colony laws if those things went against what he felt was correct. He claimed that all of his teachings were divinely inspired.

Davenport's work led to splits within churches and families. Whitefield wrote of his discoveries that his supporters "were apprehensive. . .that I would promote or encourage separations, and that some would have been encouraged to separate by my saying in my journal that I found the generality of preachers preached an unknown Christ. . . ."

Whitefield recorded his response: "I said I was sorry if anything I wrote had been a means of promoting separations, for I was of no separating principles, but came to New England to preach the gospel of peace. . .and promote charity and love among all.

"We talked freely and friendly about several things. . . by which the jealousies they had entertained concerning me seemed in a great measure ended, and Dr. Colman invited me to preach the next day at his Meeting House."

He received a similar invitation from a Dr. Webb, and this public endorsement from two respected men helped earn him a fair hearing. Over time, people's questions were answered and the vast majority of them once again supported George Whitefield.

They flocked to his meetings. So many came that he was soon preaching at both six and seven o'clock in the morning, before most people had to be at work. "My conduct and my preaching," he said, "breathed nothing but love."

Not everyone was satisfied, however. Leaders at Harvard, who had enjoyed Whitefield's ministry four years earlier, were incensed by his writings about the school in his journals. The faculty released a pamphlet called a "Testimony," dated December 28, 1744, which, among other things, charged Whitefield as being "an uncharitable, censorious, and slanderous man." They denounced his "rashness and arrogance." Whitefield responded in print to the charges. His words show that the twenty-nine-year-old preacher had learned a few things about controlling his impulsive words since he had last been in America.

"At the same time I ask pardon for any rash word I have dropped, or anything I have written or done amiss," he wrote. "This leads me also to ask forgiveness, gentlemen, if I have done you or your Society, in my Journal, any wrong.

"Be pleased to accept unfeigned thanks for all tokens of respect you showed me when here last. And if you have injured me in the 'Testimony'. . .(as I think you have) it is already forgiven, without asking, by, gentlemen, Your affectionate, humble servant, George Whitefield."

Whitefield learned from what the Harvard faculty wrote about him. "They have done me real service," he wrote in February of the next year. "Some unguarded expressions in the heat of less experienced youth I certainly did drop. I was much too precipitate in hearkening to and publishing private informations, and thereby, Peterlike, cut off too many ears. . . . May I be purged of some of my corruptions, and be kept in good temper towards those who, I believe, really think they do God's service in opposing."

The "Testimony" also raised questions about how the orphanage was being run. As a result, Whitefield decided to prepare a detailed financial report on Bethesda. He felt this would finally answer any questions about improprieties, and let those people who had donated so generously toward the orphanage know how their money was being used.

The Whitefields stayed in New England for nine months. No matter what controversies swirled around the evangelist, huge crowds flocked to hear him speak. But George Whitefield knew he was needed at Bethesda. As he prepared to leave New England for the South in August 1745, he was satisfied with the work that had been accomplished. "The Lord causes prejudices to subside," he wrote, "and makes my formerly most bitter enemies to be at peace. . . . O help me to praise Him whose mercy endureth for ever!"

As the Whitefields traveled south through New York, New Jersey, and Philadelphia, they encountered some of the same misunderstandings that had awaited them in Boston, but the situations were not nearly as difficult nor as intense as they had been in New England. A group in Philadelphia even offered to pay the evangelist eight hundred pounds per year if he would only preach for them six months a year. He declined the offer and the couple continued their journey toward Georgia.

When they reached Virginia, Elizabeth and George Whitefield were met by a striking example of the impact of the evangelist's printed sermons. Two years before, a bricklayer named Samuel Morris had begun reading copies of Whitefield's sermons to small gatherings of his neighbors. The words had an immediate impact on the people. Many were convicted of their sin and became followers of Christ.

Before long, Morris's house was too small to contain the group of people who wanted to listen to Whitefield's sermons. So they built a house to be used for the readings. Eventually, four different reading houses had to be built.

Whitefield was excited by what was happening. He stayed with the group for a few days and encouraged them in their work. Eventually, this group became the starting point of the Presbyterian Church in Virginia.

The Whitefields finally reached Bethesda sometime in late November or early December 1746. The orphanage had been transformed since George Whitefield's last visit. The building was completed and nearly three miles of wooded area had been cleared. But as usual, many problems required his immediate attention. Because the orphanage was remote, retaining staff was difficult. The superintendent, James Habersham, had resigned his position to go to Savannah. A teacher and chaplain had also resigned. Whitefield needed to hire suitable replacements. Then there were decisions about running the plantation and finishing details on the work in the buildings.

More than anything else, however, George Whitefield was concerned about the orphanage's finances. Because of the criticism about fundraising that had followed him throughout the colonies, he had refrained from asking people to donate to the orphans. Some people had given private donations on the side, but Whitefield knew he needed a more reliable source of income.

Benjamin Franklin offered to insert an appeal for the orphanage in his papers and to send it to other papers in both America and England. Whitefield vetoed that idea because he feared it would be interpreted as a lack of faith in God's ability to provide. So Franklin donated seventy-five pounds of his own money for the orphanage—more than a year's salary for a common laborer at the time.

Then friends in South Carolina purchased a plantation and slaves for the express purpose of providing money for Bethesda through its earnings. They gave the plantation to George Whitefield, and he thus became a slave owner. He named the plantation Providence.

By not objecting to slavery, Whitefield reflected the general opinions of white Christians of his day. The vast majority of ministers in America had slaves who did household work; the Quakers were about the only group to speak out against the institution in the eighteenth century. Slaves of Whitefield's time did appreciate the many things he did to improve their living conditions, but his blindness to the evils inherent in the institution remains a valid criticism today.

Throughout 1747 George Whitefield continued to preach in the colonies. Sometimes his wife traveled with him. At other times she stayed at Bethesda. Whitefield himself never made allowances for his physical condition. He had never fully recovered from his deathly illness when he first arrived in the colonies, and the heat of the oncoming summer only aggravated his weakness. By June the heat and humidity of the southern colonies was oppressive, but George Whitefield always wore his black wool clerical robe over his everyday clothes whenever he preached.

Concerned friends began warning him that he was driving himself too hard. These included Dr. William Shippen, the foremost doctor in the colonies and the brother of Philadelphia's mayor. Shippen strongly urged Whitefield to allow himself a period of rest. Whitefield refused. In a letter written to a friend in England, the evangelist said, "Here are thousands and thousands who as to spiritual things know not their right hand from their left. . . . I have been within these five weeks a circuit of 400 miles. . . . Nobody goes out scarcely but myself."

Whitefield stubbornly refused to take advice from the many people God had placed around him. He wrote to another friend, "I intend going on till I drop." He got his wish. Throughout most of the month of June, he was confined to his bed. He had a high fever and convulsions. Often people feared he was near death.

Word reached him from Boston that it would be very helpful for him to join the work throughout New England. Still very weak, Whitefield rose from his bed and set out to the north. The cooler weather helped his health improve somewhat, but he still was far from well. By the end of the year, Elizabeth and George Whitefield were once again in Philadelphia.

In March 1748 it was obvious even to the evangelist that he was in no condition to continue preaching. He agreed with Dr. Shippen's idea of traveling to Bermuda for a rest. Elizabeth Whitefield did not enjoy travel by ship. The couple agreed that she would stay in Philadelphia with friends while he went to Bermuda. When he recovered, he would return to Philadelphia, and the two of them would travel together back to England.

The plan was never carried out. In Bermuda George Whitefield was soon preaching to anyone who would listen. His report about Sunday, May 9, is typical of how he spent his time: "This also, I trust, has been a good Sabbath. In the morning I was helped to preach powerfully to a meeting, and rather a larger congregation than ever, in Mr. Paul's meeting house; and in the evening to almost as large a congregation of blacks and whites, as last Sunday in the fields, near my hearty friend's, Mr. Holiday's house. To see so many black faces was affecting. They heard very attentively and some of them now begin to weep. May God grant them a godly sorrow that needeth not to be repented of."

One of the powerful men on the island chose to raise funds for the orphanage, and the amount of money he raised greatly eased Whitefield's level of concern about that responsibility. The easing of the stress caused by Bethesda's finances, along with the fact that for once he was free from any controversy, caused his health to improve slightly in spite of his activities.

But after eleven weeks in Bermuda, George Whitefield knew it was time to leave. Howell Harris had been sending him numerous letters describing problems that were developing at the Tabernacle and among the different religious societies that looked to Whitefield for leadership. As time passed, the letters became more urgent. Rather than take a ship to Philadelphia and then travel with his wife to England, Whitefield sent word to Elizabeth that he was sailing directly for England and that she should make her own way over.

As he sailed toward England, Whitefield spent time reviewing his published journals. Eight years had passed since the last journal had been printed, and during that time he had matured and learned many things. In a letter written aboard ship, Whitefield commented, "Alas! Alas! In how many things I have judged and acted wrong. I have been too rash and hasty in giving characters, both of places and persons. Being fond of Scripture language I have often used a style too apostolical, and at the same time have been too bitter in my zeal. Wild fire has been mixed with it and. . .I frequently wrote and spoke in my own spirit, when I thought I was writing and speaking by the assistance of the Spirit of God.

"I have likewise too much made inward impressions my rule of acting, and too soon and too explicitly published what had been better kept in longer, or told after my death. By these things I have given some wrong touches to God's ark, and hurt the blessed cause I would defend, and also stirred up needless opposition. This has humbled me much. . . . I bless [God] for ripening my judgment a little more, for giving me to see and confess, and I hope in some degree to correct and amend, some of my mistakes."

With this attitude, Whitefield arrived in London in July 1748.

nine

When Whitefield returned to England, he learned that his illnesses in America had been exaggerated to the point that some people believed he was dead. Having reassured his followers that indeed he was still alive, he faced many decisions. First on his agenda was deciding what to do with the Calvinist Methodist societies. Thirty-three-year-old George Whitefield wanted to spend most of the rest of his life working in the American colonies, but the English groups he had started were without the leadership of John Cennick and John Syms, his former assistants who were now working with the Moravians. Howell Harris had done his best to keep the Calvinist Methodists together, but he was not a strong administrator.

Whitefield also sensed a competitive spirit between the Calvinist Methodists who followed him and the more Arminian Methodists who aligned themselves with John

Wesley. As he began speaking to groups in London— usually numbering more than a thousand—Whitefield sensed a desire among many of his followers for him to pack the churches and tabernacles so that they could claim triumph over the Wesleys.

Whitefield had no interest in repeating the conflicts he'd experienced with the Wesley brothers earlier in the decade, but he also realized that doctrinal differences would never allow the two groups to merge. On September 1, 1748, Whitefield wrote to John Wesley about this very subject:

> *What have you thought about a union? I am afraid an external one is impracticable. I find, by your sermons, that we differ in principles more than I thought; and I believe we are upon two different plans. My attachment to America will not permit me to abide very long in England; consequently, I should weave but a Penelope's web, if I formed Societies; and, if I should form them, I have not proper assistants to take care of them. I intend, therefore, to go about preaching the gospel to every creature. You, I suppose, are for settling Societies every- where; but more of this when we meet.*

Having seen in America how the spiritual mission of church groups could be destroyed by conflicts over personal conduct and theology, Whitefield looked for a way to keep English Methodism from tearing itself apart. He decided to remove himself from the leadership of the Calvinistic societies, a decision that was formalized later in a London meeting of the Calvinist Methodists held on April 27, 1749. The men attending agreed that Howell Harris would take over the leadership of the London Tabernacle and the other Calvinistic societies in England, and that Whitefield would support the movement by preaching the gospel both in England and abroad. For the rest of his life, Whitefield emphasized a broadly based evangelistic ministry to any group that would work with him. This left John Wesley as the one acknowledged leader of the larger Methodist movement.

Whitefield was unable to find men to replace him as the leader of some of the older, established groups in England, Wales, and Scotland. These groups felt a personal connection with the young preacher and were unwilling to break that relationship. While he remained involved with these groups for the rest of his life, he refused to start any new Calvinistic societies.

Instead, in partnership with the Countess of Huntingdon, George Whitefield began to work within the Church of England to bring about reform. This was not surprising, because he had always remained loyal to the liturgy and sacramental theology of the established church. As time passed, Whitefield found more opportunities for evangelistic work among the parishes of the Church of England. At the same time, his followers and those they influenced advocated important evangelical reforms. Whitefield's Calvinist Methodist societies began to influence English society through the Church of England, even as Wesley's Methodist societies moved away from it.

Choosing to break away from the Methodist movement and work within the established church may have been a major decision, but Whitefield came to it quickly. Less than two months after he returned to England, his ministry had made two fundamental shifts. He had decided to preach to anyone who would listen, rather than exclusively ministering to the Calvinist Methodist societies, and he also gained financial stability when the Countess of Huntingdon made him her personal chaplain.

The countess wanted to do anything she could to bring her aristocratic friends into a personal relationship with Jesus. With Whitefield as her chaplain, she could invite them to listen to him in the privacy of her home, rather than in the public venue of the tabernacles and churches. She sensed that many members of the aristocracy would be less resistant to Whitefield's words when surrounded by a group of their peers rather than when on public display. Many members of the aristocracy viewed themselves as superior to commoners and were not likely to admit to failings while surrounded by people they identified as their subordinates. In a letter dated August 21, 1748, Whitefield showed his support of the countess's goals:

> *I received your ladyship's letter late last night. I am quite willing to comply with your invitation. As I am to preach at St. Bartholomew's on Wednesday evening, I will wait upon your ladyship the next morning, and spend the whole day at Chelsea. Blessed be God, that the rich and great begin to have a hearing ear. Surely your ladyship and Madam Edwin are only the firstfruits. A word in the lesson, when I was last at your ladyship's struck me—"Paul preached privately to those who*

were of reputation." This must be the way, I pre-sume, of dealing with the nobility who yet know not the Lord. O that I may be enabled so to preach as to win their souls to the blessed Jesus!

By September 1, in a communication with a friend, Whitefield described his work in England with these words:

My hands have been full of work, and I have been among great company. A privy counsellor of the King of Denmark, and others, with one of the Prince of Wales's favourites, dined and drank tea with me on Monday. On Tuesday, I preached twice at Lady Huntingdon's, to several of the nobility. In the morning, the Earl of Chesterfield was present. In the evening, Lord Bolingbroke. All behaved quite well, and were in some degree affected. Lord Chesterfield thanked me, and said, "Sir, I will not tell you what I shall tell others, how I approve of you," or words to this purpose. He conversed with me freely afterwards. Lord Bolingbroke was much moved, and desired I would come and see him next morning. I did, and his lordship behaved with great candour and frankness. All accepted of my sermons. Thus, my dear brother, the world turns round. "In all time of my wealth, good Lord, deliver me!"

Through the influence of Lady Huntingdon, George Whitefield developed relationships with some of the most important businessmen and politicians in England. This was a marked change from his days as a student at Oxford when he could not speak to the aristocracy unless spoken to first. Most of these influential people were impressed with the young preacher. Lord Bolingbroke wrote to the Countess of Huntingdon: "Mr. Whitefield is the most extraordinary man in our times. He has the most commanding eloquence I ever heard in any person; his abilities are very considerable; his zeal unquenchable; and his piety and excellence genuine—unquestionable. The bishops and inferior orders of clergy are very angry with him, and endeavour to represent him as a hypocrite, an enthusiast; but this is not astonishing—there is so little real goodness or honesty among them."

Lord Chesterfield was another member of the aristocracy who was impressed by Whitefield's skills. Known as a great orator himself, he said, "Mr. Whitefield's eloquence is unrivalled—his zeal inexhaustible; and not to admire both would argue a total absence of taste."

Even those opposed to Christianity admitted that Whitefield had unique gifts. David Hume, known for his agnosticism, judged that "Mr. Whitefield is the most ingenious preacher I ever heard. It is worth going twenty miles to hear him."

Whitefield did not intend to stay in London. In September 1748 he headed for Scotland, arriving in Edinburgh on Wednesday, September 14. After his recent experience in London—his warm welcome and his appointment as chaplain for the Countess of Huntingdon—Scotland was somewhat of a shock. To begin with, many of Whitefield's friends had died since his last visit. Other friends he described as backsliders, and some of the ministers were, in Whitefield's view, "shy." The weather was harsh, and Whitefield started losing his voice. Two weeks into his stay in Scotland, he wrote, "I have met with some unexpected rubs, but not one more than was necessary to humble my proud heart."

One of those "rubs" occurred when members of the Synod of Glasgow had a long debate about him, including unsubstantiated charges that the money he raised for the orphans in Georgia never reached them. Then the Presbytery of Perth decided against letting him preach. Whitefield carefully avoided those things that would inflame his critics. During the six weeks he spent in Scotland, he refused to take public offerings or speak about the financial needs of the orphanage in Georgia, even though it concerned him greatly. The general public continued to turn out for his sermons, and he preached every day, usually in the Orphan Hospital Park in Edinburgh. By the time he left Scotland at the end of October, organized opposition to him in that country had reached an end.

As soon as Whitefield returned to London in the beginning of November, he began preaching twice a week at the Countess of Huntingdon's home. While there, he received a letter from Howell Harris describing Harris's work in Wales. Whitefield's friend had traveled 150 miles a week and preached at least twice a day for nine weeks. During his travels he had tried to avoid contact with Sir Watkin William Wynn, a Welsh baronet who was known for his hatred of Methodists. Harris wasn't entirely successful. A few days before writing his letter to Whitefield, he reported, Sir Watkin Wynn had forced Methodists to pay fines varying from five shillings to twenty pounds, simply because they were meeting together. Mobs disrupted the meetings, and near the town of Bala, someone hit Harris on the head with such force that his head almost split open.

Immediately after Whitefield read Harris's letter, he told the Countess of Huntingdon what was happening in Wales. She used her political connections to persuade the government to force Sir Watkin Wynn to return all the fines he had taken from the Methodists.

Late in November Isaac Watts, the famous hymn writer, was close to death. An article published in *Gospel Magazine* twenty-eight years later reported that Whitefield visited Watts on November 25, 1748, the day the hymn writer died. When Whitefield asked Watts how he was doing, Watts responded, "I am one of Christ's waiting servants." Then Whitefield helped the older man sit up in bed so that he could more easily swallow his medicine. When Watts apologized for causing such trouble, Whitefield replied, "Surely, I am not too good to wait on a waiting servant of Christ." About thirty minutes after Whitefield left Watts's home, the musician died. Whether the meeting actually took place—and many sources doubt that the story is authentic—it is clear that Whitefield valued the contributions Isaac Watts had made to the Methodist movement. He made use of Watts's hymns throughout his ministry.

In early December Whitefield traveled to Gloucester and Bristol for meetings. While there, he became increasingly concerned about the orphanage in Georgia. He had been unable to convince anyone in England to go to Georgia and work in the orphanage, but he desperately wanted it to become a seminary that would provide the southern colonies with ministers. He received word that his wife was about to return to England and that the trustees, wanting to solve their financial problems, were thinking of taking on slaves, although slavery was still illegal in the Georgia colony.

On December 6, 1748, writing from Gloucester, Whitefield told the trustees that he thought the use of slavery would provide the best solution, but he stressed that he didn't want slaves used until it could be done legally. He went so far as to say that if slaves or indentured servants were not introduced soon, he could not promise to continue the orphanage in any significant way. While Whitefield did much to improve conditions for slaves in the American colonies, he also failed to see the immorality of owning another human being.

By the middle of December, Whitefield returned to London at the Countess of Huntingdon's request. There he resumed speaking at her home and preaching at the Tabernacle. After the first of the year, he once again started traveling through western England, preaching to thousands of people at a time. He also learned of some results from his preaching a few years earlier. In Kingsbridge he was told that a young man he had led to Christ at that time was now a pastor. Whitefield vividly remembered how the young man had climbed a tree to ridicule him during a sermon. Whitefield had called up to the heckler, telling him to imitate Zaccheus and come down from the tree to receive the Lord Jesus. "The word was backed with power," Whitefield recalled. "He heard, came down, believed, and now adorns the gospel."

As spring approached, Whitefield returned to London. On the way, he crossed paths with Charles Wesley and learned that his friend was planning an April wedding with Sarah Gwynne, the daughter of an affluent man who lived in south Wales. The young couple shared their faith in Christ and similar social positions. In eighteenth-century England, comparable social rank within a marriage was considered very important. Sarah proved to be a gracious and talented woman, and she and Charles were very happy together. In a society where many members of the upper classes married to improve family connections or wealth, such happiness was not the expected outcome of marriage.

The Countess of Huntingdon kept Whitefield quite busy preaching to the aristocracy, but he still made time for anyone who wanted to know about God, no matter what their social standing. *The Life and Times of the Countess of Huntingdon* recounts the story of some of the countess's friends questioning Whitefield's views of the poor. "Among other preposterous things," the ladies reported to the countess, "he declared that Jesus Christ is so willing to receive sinners, that He does not object to receive even the devil's castaways! My lady, did you ever hear of such a thing since you were born?" These members of the aristocracy were appalled that the young preacher would imply that in God's view, poor commoners were on an equal footing with the nobility.

The countess agreed that Whitefield's words were unusual, but because he was in her house at the time, she suggested that she send for him and let him explain his words. When Whitefield heard the story, he agreed that he had said what was reported and then related what had brought about his statement. A poor, miserable woman had asked to speak with him and told him that the evening before she had happened to pass by the chapel door when Whitefield was preaching.

"One of the first things I heard you say was that Jesus Christ was so willing to receive sinners that He did not object to receiving the devil's castaways," the poor woman said. "Now, sir, I have been on the town many years, and am so worn out in his service, that I think I may with truth be called one of the devil's castaways. Do you think, sir, that Jesus Christ would receive me?"

Whitefield paused and looked at the countess and her friends. "I assured her there was not a doubt of it," he said, "if she was but willing to go to Him."

By the middle of May, Whitefield was set to leave for Wales. Not only was he looking forward to preaching, but in June he planned on being reunited with his wife in the small English town of Abergavenny, located on the Welsh border. He also had a surprise for her. During her absence from Britain he had supervised the building of a home for them next to the London Tabernacle. The "Tabernacle House," as he named it, became their base of operations for the rest of their lives. Their reunion lasted for two days, a time, Whitefield said, of "sweet, very sweet retirement—so sweet that I should be glad never to be heard of again. But this must not be. A necessity is laid upon me; and woe is me if I preach not the gospel of Christ."

Whitefield spent much of the rest of the year traveling to Wales and parts of England from his base in London. In early October he once again became involved with the

Wesley brothers. Charles had learned that his brother John had made an agreement known as a *spousal de praesenti* with a young widow named Grace Murray. Earlier in the century, such an agreement meant that the parties were in effect married but that the consummation of that marriage would take place after the religious wedding ceremony. By 1749, however, a *spousal de praesenti* did not carry the same legal weight. Charles was appalled that his brother would consider marrying a woman who, however devout, was several stations beneath him in the social order. He decided to act quickly to prevent what in his mind would be a disaster.

Charles convinced Mrs. Murray that she should marry a young preacher named John Bennet, to whom she had previously been engaged. Charles told Whitefield what he was doing and sent a letter to his brother John, asking him to meet Charles and Whitefield in the town of Leeds. When John arrived in Leeds, Charles wasn't there. It fell to Whitefield to tell John that Charles was performing the wedding ceremony of Grace Murray and John Bennet. Understandably, John Wesley was devastated. He truly loved Grace and felt that their agreement bound them together as husband and wife. Then news came that Grace Murray and John Bennet were in fact married. When Charles and the newly married couple arrived in Leeds, John at first refused to speak to his brother. Whitefield and another friend, John Nelson, begged John Wesley to reconsider his position. They prayed together with him and spoke of the need for forgiveness. In the end, the Wesley brothers were reunited. Three days later Charles Wesley wrote a letter in which he stated, "George Whitefield, and my brother, and I, are one—a threefold cord which shall no more be broken."

As 1750 began, George Whitefield followed similar patterns. He traveled throughout England, Wales, and Scotland, but maintained a base in London. The Countess of Huntingdon continued to support him financially and to introduce him to members of the aristocracy. One change was that Whitefield frequently was invited to preach in the Wesley brothers' churches and meetings. He also continued corresponding with people in the American colonies, including Benjamin Franklin. But illness stubbornly remained a problem, particularly when he spent time in the city of London, where the smoky air probably aggravated Whitefield's respiratory problems.

By December of that year, Whitefield was bedridden with a serious illness that he described simply as a "violent fever." For almost two weeks he was unable to leave his room. His gradual recovery was immediately followed by the serious illness of both his wife and the Countess of Huntingdon. The countess, who had been seriously ill throughout December, became so ill at the beginning of the new year that her household feared she would die. Whitefield received a message asking him to hurry to the countess's home in Ashby. By the time he reached the estate, Lady Huntingdon was still alive, but her sister-in-law, Lady Frances Hastings, had died. Whitefield found almost every member of the household ill, and stayed to help for several days after Lady Hastings's funeral.

When he returned to London, he found his wife "exceeding bad." While there is no clear record of what happened, it is known that she was expecting a child.

Most historians conclude that, like their previous child, the Whitefields' baby was born dead or died shortly after birth. Mrs. Whitefield slowly recovered, but neither she nor her husband were in good health that winter.

During March 1751 Whitefield traveled to Bristol where the Countess of Huntingdon was recovering from her illness. While there, he learned that slavery had been made legal in Georgia. On March 22 he wrote a letter to a minister in the American colonies which included these thoughts about slavery:

> *As to the lawfulness of keeping slaves, I have no doubt, since I hear of some that were bought with Abraham's money, and some that were born in his house. I, also, cannot help thinking, that some of those servants mentioned by the apostles, in their epistles, were or had been slaves. . . . Though liberty is a sweet thing to such as are born free, yet to those who never knew the sweets of it, slavery perhaps may not be so irksome.*
>
> *However this be, it is plain to a demonstration, that hot countries cannot be cultivated without [black slaves]. What a flourishing country might Georgia have been, had the use of them been permitted years ago! How many white people have been destroyed for want of them, and how many thousands of pounds spent to no purpose at all! . . .And, though it is true that they are brought in a wrong way from their native country, and it is a trade not to be approved of, yet, as it will be carried on whether*

we will or not, I should think myself highly favoured if I could purchase a good number of them, to make their lives comfortable, and lay a foundation for breeding up their posterity in the nurture and admonition of the Lord.

You know, dear sir, that I had no hand in bringing them into Georgia. Though my judgment was for it, and so much money was yearly spent to no purpose, and I was strongly importuned thereto, yet I would have no [slave] upon my plantation, till the use of them was publicly allowed in the colony. Now this is done, let us reason no more about it, but diligently improve the present opportunity for their instruction. The Trustees favour it, and we may never have a like prospect. It rejoiced my soul, to hear that one of my poor [slaves] in Carolina was made a brother in Christ. How know we but we may have many such instances in Georgia before long? By mixing with your people, I trust many of them will be brought to Jesus; and this consideration, as to us, swallows up all temporal inconveniences whatsoever.

Whitefield's rationalizations of slavery are morally repugnant to Christians today, but unfortunately, they represent views held by most white Christians of his time.

By the end of May 1751, Whitefield left by ship for Ireland. He arrived in Dublin on May 24 and immediately began preaching to huge crowds. Traveling to cities with well-established Methodist societies, Whitefield preached several times a day for weeks. He had never fully recovered from the fever of the previous winter, and his letters during his travels in Ireland are full of references to more health problems. On June 10 he wrote from Athlone to the Countess of Huntingdon, "As the weather grows warmer, my body grows weaker, and my vomitings follow me continually." A week later, writing from Limerick, he stated, "Everywhere, our Lord has vouchsafed us His blessed presence. This supports me under the heat of the weather, the weakness of my body, and the various trials which exercise my mind."

Whitefield preached to crowds of thousands, and no matter how badly he felt, he pushed on. Several letters mention preaching five, six, or seven times in one day. In the middle of July Whitefield left Ireland for Scotland. Here, again, he kept a grueling schedule. Because he faced none of the criticisms that had marked other visits to Scotland, Whitefield felt free to raise money for Bethesda.

While Whitefield preached in Ireland and Scotland, his wife remained behind in London. She, too, faced continuing health problems. In a letter she wrote to the Countess of Huntingdon on July 13, Mrs. Whitefield apologized for not writing sooner: "I have been so ill since I came home, that Dr. Lobb and Dr. Nisbett have attended me more or less, ever since. I was in bed when I received your ladyship's letter, and was not able to read it. I had a pleuritic fever, and was so low that the doctor durst not bleed me. I am glad to hear, by Mr. Smith, that your ladyship is so well. God be praised! O may the good Lord give your ladyship a prosperous soul in a healthy body, to His own glory, and the good of very many poor souls!"

By the time George Whitefield was ready to leave

Scotland, he was satisfied with his accomplishments and eager to set sail for the American colonies. In an August 10 letter to the Countess of Huntingdon, Whitefield reported, "The longer I stayed at Edinburgh, the more eagerly both rich and poor attended on the word preached. For near twenty-eight days, in Glasgow and Edinburgh, I preached to near ten thousand souls every day." In that same letter, he noted, "I threw up much blood in Edinburgh, but riding recruits me."

While Whitefield himself tended to ignore his body's well-being, friends as diverse as the devotedly secular Ben Franklin and the devout Christian Robert Cruttenden repeatedly expressed concern for the preacher's health. On August 29, 1751, Whitefield left England aboard the *Antelope*. He was bound for Georgia and was taking several poor children with him. The next day his friend Cruttenden wrote in a letter, "Yesterday I took leave of Mr. Whitefield, who is embarked for America, with little prospect of my ever seeing him again. His constitution is quite worn out with labour." As Whitefield's nineteenth-century biographer Luke Tyerman observed, "It was fortunate that he got away. Without this, he probably would have died. The man was fast becoming a sort of religious suicide. Humanly speaking, his voyage to America saved, or rather prolonged, his life."[1] George Whitefield was only thirty-six years old.

ten

W hen George Whitefield left England in August 1751, he intended to stay in America for quite some time. During the voyage he started reworking his journals, desiring to temper some of the more extreme material in the originals. The *Antelope* landed in Savannah in October, and Whitefield took the children he had brought with him to Bethesda. Very little is known about this trip to America. It is clear that he intended to spend some time on business affairs at the orphanage. He also desperately needed to give his body a chance to recover some health. From the few surviving letters that he wrote during his visit, we know that he did some preaching and was encouraged by the condition of the orphans at Bethesda. He also learned that his friend Dr. Philip Doddridge had died.

Dr. Doddridge was a well-respected evangelical minister, theologian, and writer of hymns; he had been an early supporter of Whitefield's work. His devotional classic, *The Rise and Progress of Religion in the Soul,* which had appeared in 1745, had already had a profound impact on Whitefield, the Wesleys, and many other Christian leaders, both in Britain and in America.

The surviving letters also indicate that Whitefield planned on making a preaching tour through the colonies during the spring of 1752. Those plans, however, were abruptly canceled in March when he suddenly left for England. Two situations caused this precipitous action. First, Whitefield got news that Georgia had become a royal colony, and he wanted to secure some privileges for the orphanage before the original charter expired. Second, he was receiving reports that John Wesley's publication of "Serious Thoughts upon the Perseverance of the Saints" had stirred up conflict once again between Calvinist and Arminian Methodists. This time, the focus of the controversy was the issue of eternal security for believers. Calvinists believed that the eternal destiny of all believers was secured by the sovereign act of God in redeeming them. John Wesley was no longer sure that this was true. He had come to believe that without regular, visible spiritual growth, a believer's salvation might erode and eventually be lost.

Whitefield had learned through painful experience how destructive such conflicts could become. He felt it would be prudent to return to England and calm some of the Calvinist pastors. As he wrote in a letter from America:

> *All truths, unless productive of holiness and love, are of no avail. They may float upon the surface of the understanding; but this is to no*

purpose, unless they transform the heart. I trust, the dear Tabernacle preachers will always have this deeply impressed upon their minds. Let us not dispute, but love. Truth is great, and will prevail. I am quite willing that all our hearers shall hear for themselves. The spirit of Christ is a spirit of liberty. Let us look above names and parties. Let Jesus, the ever-loving, the ever-lovely Jesus, be our all in all. So that He be preached, and His Divine image stamped more and more upon people's souls, I care not who is uppermost. I know my place, (Lord Jesus, enable me to keep it!) even to be the servant of all. I want not to have a people called after my name, and, therefore, I act as I do. The cause is Christ's, and He will take care of it.

When he reached England, Whitefield was greeted with the news that his mother had died while he was in America. Strange as it may seem, the news did not stop him from returning to London and immersing himself in preaching. His relationship with his mother had been strained and distant ever since his spiritual crisis when he was a student at Oxford. Though Whitefield kept in contact with her by letter, what he wrote showed more concern for her spiritual well-being than for her material needs or physical health. Whatever grief he may have felt at her death, he did not allow it to keep him from carrying on his work.

After spending about a month in London, Whitefield left for Portsmouth and then Bath. Many of the aristocracy were spending the summer months near Bath, as was their custom, and Whitefield spent three weeks there with the Countess of Huntingdon. She arranged that each evening he would preach to large groups of the nobility, including Mrs. Grinfield, a lady who attended Queen Caroline.

In the middle of July Whitefield left for Wales. Within two weeks he traveled three hundred miles and preached twenty times. He also attended several Associations, as meetings of Methodist leaders and society members were called. Why was a man who had committed himself to staying free of ties to specific movements becoming involved in the Calvinistic Methodist Societies? The answer involves difficulties that developed with Howell Harris.

Four years earlier, when Whitefield had relinquished his official roles within the Calvinist Methodist movement, Harris had been asked to take over the leadership of the Tabernacle in London. Harris was already exhausted from years of pushing himself to do more than his body was able. The new responsibilities of leadership taxed his strength even more.

Then during an outdoor meeting in northern Wales, Harris was hit on the head with what he described as "violence enough to slit my head in two." At the time, Harris said that he wasn't hurt, but after that incident, his behavior changed. He became paranoid and unpredictable. One day he would describe a person in glowing terms. The next day that person would be despicable. He began to teach that God the Father died at Calvary, and he did not tolerate anyone contradicting his teachings because he so strongly believed that his teachings were directly from God.

His changed behavior, taken with reports in his diary of "unbearable headache," "excruciating pains in my head," and "feeling that my brain is almost turning," indicate that Harris had suffered some type of head injury from the attack. But because of limited medical knowledge, it appears that no one considered that Harris might not be responsible for his behavior. Churches no longer allowed him to preach, and by 1752 he had retreated to his home in Trevecka, where he was joined by loyal followers.

The situation created a great deal of turmoil and conflict among laypeople. Apparently, Whitefield decided it was important that he attend Associations throughout that summer to help restore stability and unity to the movement. In a letter he wrote on August 1 while in Bristol, he stated, "In my way hither, we held an Association. There were present about nine clergy, and near forty other labourers. I trust all of them are born of God, and desirous to promote His glory, and His people's good. All was harmony and love."

Whitefield was personally distressed by Harris's condition. Howell Harris had been one of his closest friends. As active in evangelism as Whitefield, Harris understood stresses that Whitefield faced in ways few other people could. Fortunately, after two years of complete rest, Harris began to recover. More than 150 followers eventually lived at Trevecka in a communal arrangement, similar to Moravian institutions.

In August 1752 Whitefield made his way back to London for a short stay. While there, he wrote a letter to his friend Ben Franklin, congratulating him on the fame he was achieving in Europe as a result of his experiments with electricity. As always, he took the opportunity to insert some lines encouraging his friend to be equally diligent in studying spiritual issues:

I find that you grow more and more famous in the learned world. As you have made a pretty considerable progress in the mysteries of electricity, I would now humbly recommend to your diligent unprejudiced pursuit and study the mystery of the new birth. It is a most important, interesting study, and, when mastered, will richly repay you for all your pains. One, at whose bar we are shortly to appear, hath solemnly declared, that, without it, "we cannot enter into the kingdom of heaven." You will excuse this freedom.

Shortly after writing this letter, Whitefield traveled to Scotland. He visited many of the places where he had preached in the past, including Edinburgh and Glasgow. Near the end of the tour, he sent a letter to the Countess of Huntingdon. He summarized his experiences in this way: "For about twenty-eight days, I suppose, I did not preach, in Scotland, to less than ten thousand every day. This has weakened my body; but the Redeemer knows how to renew my strength. I am as well as a pilgrim can expect to be. About £70 were collected for the Edinburgh Orphans; and I heard of near a dozen young men, who were awakened about ten years ago, and have since entered the ministry, and are likely to prove very useful. Praise the Lord, O my soul!"

As typically happened, Whitefield ignored his physical problems and continued preaching throughout England. On November 3 he reported in a letter, "I have been upwards of three weeks from Scotland, and scarce ever had more encouragement in preaching the everlasting gospel. At Newcastle, Sunderland, and several places in Yorkshire, Lancashire, and Cheshire, thousands and thousands have daily attended on the word preached. I hear that arrows have stuck fast in many hearts. I am returning to Leeds; and, from thence, I shall go to York, and to several places in Lincolnshire, and am to preach at Sheffield next Lord's-day. My return to London must be determined by the weather. It has been uncommonly favourable; and it is a pity to go into winter quarters, so long as work can be done in the fields. O that I had as many tongues as there are hairs upon my head! Jesus should have them all."

Within a week Whitefield was back in London. The unrelenting pressure of his summer and fall schedule had finally caught up with him. "My Sunday's work," he wrote, "sickness, the change of weather, and parting from friends, so enfeebled me, that I was in hopes, on the road, my imprisoned soul would have been set at liberty, and fled to the blissful regions. I found my poor wife an invalid. Our Lord can restore her, for He came to heal our sicknesses, and to bear our infirmities."

In point of fact, Elizabeth Whitefield's repeated miscarriages had left her a semi-invalid. She lived the remainder of her life in London, unable to join her husband in any of his travels through Great Britain or across the Atlantic.

As the new year began, George Whitefield had two projects on his mind. The first was arranging to have Providence, his South Carolina plantation, sold as soon as possible. He had decided that he needed to concentrate his efforts in the New World, and that it would be much better to dispose of the plantation and turn the proceeds back into the Georgia orphanage. On January 7, 1753, he sent a power of attorney to a friend in America, asking him to sell the property. "I would only observe," he wrote, "that I had rather it should be sold for less than its real value, than to keep it any longer in my hands. I do not choose to keep two families longer than is necessary. The money you receive from Providence will be immediately wanted to buy more land, and to pay for opening Bethesda's new plantation."

The second project was to raise money to build a new tabernacle in London. The old one had never been more than an ugly shed, and after surviving a dozen winters, it obviously needed to be replaced. The project was supported by the Countess of Huntingdon as well as Lady Frances Shirley, but Whitefield was determined not to begin building until he had raised a thousand pounds toward the cost. With the help of his well-connected friends, it didn't take long to get the necessary funding. On March 1, 1753, the first brick was laid, and within fifteen weeks the tabernacle was open to worshipers.

While the construction activity was in full swing, Whitefield was also preparing a "small collection of hymns for public worship." Entitled "Hymns for Social Worship, collected from various Authors, and more particularly designed for the use of the Tabernacle congregation in London," the hymnbook was a great success. It included 170 hymns and several short doxologies. The vast majority of the hymns were by Isaac Watts, but the book also included twenty-one hymns by John and

Charles Wesley. Between 1753 and 1796 Whitefield's hymnbook reportedly went through thirty-six editions.

That same spring Whitefield decided he had to release a public statement separating himself from the Moravians. Over the years, Whitefield had been closely connected with this group of German pietists—in fact, some people thought he had joined them. But since 1745 he and other figures, such as the Wesley brothers, had become increasingly concerned about some practices that were becoming part of Moravian life and worship. To begin with, many Moravians, following the teachings of one of their leaders, Count Zinzendorf, believed that the Bible contained both truth and error. They also placed so much emphasis on Jesus' physical sufferings on the cross that they ignored His spiritual sufferings. The group began to disparage the use of one's intellect and went deeply into debt with little thought about how such debts were going to be repaid. Members were encouraged to loan all their possessions to the church, and some people were going bankrupt because they had loaned everything to the church and the church had not repaid them.

Then in 1752 a 177-page pamphlet attacked Zinzendorf, charging the Moravians with immoral behavior. While those charges were spurious, they appeared alongside other charges widely known to be true, so many people believed the false charges as well. At this point, Whitefield became concerned that the charges being levied against the Moravians would also harm other groups of Christians. He felt it was time to speak out so that the general public would understand that he was not endorsing the behavior now associated with the

Moravians. His pamphlet was dated April 24, 1753, and was titled "An Expostulatory Letter, addressed to Nicholas Lewis, Count Zinzendorf, and Lord Advocate of the Unita Fratrum." He addressed each point of Moravian practice that he disagreed with, gave several specific examples, and explained why he thought the practices were in error. The pamphlet was a sensation. Reproduced entirely or in part in newspapers and magazines, it gained a wide hearing. Some Moravians called Whitefield a liar and attacked him in print, but his pamphlet clearly helped to provoke changes in Moravian policies. Over time, the Moravians eliminated some of their more extreme practices and began to pay back their debts.

During the rest of the year, Whitefield preached in England, Wales, and Scotland, continuing to use London as his home base. But in November he became involved in one more building project. The Countess of Huntingdon had been raising funds to build a tabernacle in Bristol since 1749. While John Wesley had a tabernacle in Bristol, the countess understood that many of her aristocratic friends would never darken the door of a building connected with John Wesley. Because he operated outside the established Church of England, he was too controversial for them to be associated with. Construction of the countess's tabernacle was completed in the fall of 1753, and Whitefield was asked to preach at the dedication services on November 25.

About that same time John Wesley became gravely ill in London. Most of his friends and family members expected him to die, and Charles went to London to be with his brother. Then Charles's wife, who was in Bristol, contracted small pox and became quite ill herself.

The Countess of Huntingdon asked Whitefield to return to London and keep in contact with John Wesley so that Charles could be with his sick wife. Whitefield agreed and sent letters to Bristol so that Charles and the countess would know how John Wesley was doing. By the end of the year, both patients were recovering, and Whitefield spent the first part of 1754 preaching in London and preparing for his fifth trip to America. He planned on leaving in March with another group of orphans. He could hardly wait to see what was happening at the orphanage in Georgia.

eleven

George Whitefield left his frail wife in their London home and on March 7, 1754, boarded a ship for America. He took with him another group of orphans, which various sources number at between ten and twenty-two. About nine days after setting sail, the ship dropped anchor in the harbor of Lisbon, Portugal, where it stayed for a month.

An English businessman who lived in Lisbon welcomed Whitefield as his guest. The famous preacher spoke no Portuguese, so he could not hold services. This meant that, for once, Whitefield was forced to get the rest he so desperately needed. The nineteenth-century biographer Luke Tyerman suggests that Whitefield didn't preach in Lisbon because it would have put him at risk of expulsion or imprisonment, but the fact remains that very few of the roughly 350,000 inhabitants of the city spoke fluent English.

He did take the opportunity, however, to observe the Roman Catholic Holy Week activities. These included street processions and reenactments of the crucifixion of Jesus and the life and death of St. Francis of Assisi. Whitefield wrote several letters at the time, describing what he saw. He had mixed feelings. As always, he suspected that the pageantry was a hollow show rather than a legitimate expression of internal spiritual commitments.

"Vast are the outward preparations made here," he wrote in one letter. "Altars upon altars are erecting. Penitents upon penitents are. . .lashing themselves: but what I want to have erected and adorned, is an altar in my heart, and the blows and lashes I desire to feel, are the crucifixion and mortification of the old man and his deeds. Without this all is mere parade."

His beliefs about the errors of Roman Catholic teaching and the need for the Reformation were reinforced. "Every day," he wrote, "I have seen or heard something that has a tendency to make me thankful for the glorious Reformation. . . . O with what a power from on high must those glorious reformers have been endued, who dared first openly to oppose and to stem such a torrent of superstition and spiritual tyranny! And what gratitude we owe to those who, under God, were instrumental in saving England from a return of such spiritual tyranny! And what gratitude we owe to those who, under God, were instrumental in saving England from a return of such spiritual slavery, and such blind obedience to the papal power!"

But Whitefield also was impressed with the impact that the unfolding drama had on the crowds of people who participated. "The preachers here have also taught me something," he wrote. "Their action is graceful. . . . Surely our English preachers would do well to be a little more fervent in their address. They have truth on their side; why should superstition and falsehood run away with all that is pathetic and affecting?"

Whitefield's stay in Lisbon came to an end on Saturday, April 13, when his ship left the harbor and set sail for America. The voyage lasted six weeks and was unusually pleasant. They landed in South Carolina on May 26, 1754, and Whitefield took his orphans immediately to Bethesda. Between the time he had spent in Lisbon and the time he had spent on board ship, Whitefield had gone eleven straight weeks without preaching. Not since the beginning of his ministry had he faced such a long period of relative inactivity. It was no surprise, then, that he arrived in America in much better health than he had experienced for years.

Whitefield's visit at Bethesda increased his good spirits. As he had hoped, the introduction of slaves to the orphanage had increased its productivity. He dealt with questions about buildings, management, and personnel issues, and then George Whitefield turned his attention to the North. He apparently wanted another chance to take the trip he had planned but had been forced to cancel during his previous visit.

In mid-July he boarded the *Deborah*, a coastal vessel bound for New York. During that trip, he wrote a letter to Charles Wesley, in which he reported, "My health is wonderfully preserved. My wonted vomitings have left me, and though I ride whole nights, and have frequently been exposed to great thunders, violent lightnings and heavy rains, yet I am rather better than usual."

This respite from health problems did not last. As soon as Whitefield landed in New York and word of his arrival spread, he was showered with invitations to preach. A letter he wrote on July 30 gives some idea of the schedule he was keeping: "Tomorrow, God willing, I preach at Newark; on Wednesday, at New Brunswick; and hope to reach Trent Town that night. . . . Yesterday, I preached thrice: this morning I feel it. Welcome weariness for Jesus!"

He tried to conserve his strength somewhat by traveling in a chaise rather than riding a horse. But after a week in Philadelphia, he became quite ill. "Yesterday, I was taken with a violent cholera morbus," he wrote on August 7, "and hoped, ere now, to have been where the inhabitants shall no more say, 'I am sick.' " Although he was sick enough to wish at times that he were dead, Whitefield continued to push himself. On August 15 he wrote, "My late sickness, though violent, has not been unto death. With some difficulty, I can preach once a day."

At times it seemed that George Whitefield longed for death. Though he believed in the doctrine of salvation by faith and had been transformed by his experience of the new birth, Whitefield never seemed to believe that God had accepted him unconditionally. To him, holiness was necessary for salvation to be real, but holiness could only be achieved by relentless activity. No matter how much he did, he could not escape the feeling that God demanded more. This was the same works-oriented, legalistic trap that had nearly killed him during his years at Oxford.

It is one of the greatest and saddest ironies of George

Whitefield's life that he, who was more responsible than anyone else in his day for preaching the new birth, would so often pursue a "godly" death, as if it were his only real hope of salvation.

While in Philadelphia, Whitefield preached at the Academy. Located in a building originally constructed to give Whitefield a place to preach when he had visited Philadelphia back in 1740, the building, at Benjamin Franklin's suggestion, had become a school. Whitefield served as one of the trustees and made suggestions about curriculum. Eventually, the Academy evolved into the University of Pennsylvania.

In the third week of September, Whitefield was invited to speak at the commencement exercises of The College of New Jersey at Prince Town (now Princeton University). As a sign of how far the American Colonies were from the furor over the Great Awakening in the early 1740s, the officials of the college used the occasion to award George Whitefield an honorary Master of Arts degree, which he accepted but did not use.

By 1754 the huge growth in American churches caused by the Great Awakening had slowed significantly. But Whitefield was still able to attract huge crowds wherever he went. He left New Jersey and traveled into New England. He preached in Rhode Island, where he had never been before, five times. Hundreds gathered to hear him. Then he moved on to Boston where hundreds of people lined the streets, waiting for the famous preacher to arrive. While in Boston Whitefield preached at four different churches. Even when services were held at seven A.M., three thousand people would cram into the building to hear him. At one service, so many people were jammed into the building and crowded around it that the only way Whitefield could get inside to preach was to climb through a window.

By October Whitefield was feeling well enough to again travel on horseback. He rode into New Hampshire and preached two to three times a day before thousands of listeners. Then he started making his way back toward Georgia, intending to preach all the way along the more than two-thousand-mile journey.

Christmas Day, 1754, found George Whitefield a guest at Bohemia Manor in Maryland. During his travels throughout the colonies, he had often slept rolled up in a blanket on the floor. But this time Whitefield enjoyed luxurious accommodations. Bohemia Manor was a twenty-four-thousand-acre estate originally granted by Lord Baltimore. When Whitefield visited the estate, it was owned by an elderly widow named Mrs. Bayard. Well-connected with rich and powerful families in both Maryland and New York, Mrs. Bayard was also well-educated. She spoke several languages, studied Greek and Latin, and was a devout Christian.

Whitefield thoroughly enjoyed his visit with Mrs. Bayard and her family, but his frequent illnesses affected his view of how much longer he had to live. He mentioned some of those thoughts in a letter he wrote to the Countess of Huntingdon from Bohemia on December 27:

> *I am now forty years of age, and would gladly spend the day in retirement and deep humiliation before that Jesus, for whom I have done so little, though He has done and*

141

suffered so much for me.

About February, I hope to reach Georgia; and, at spring, to embark for England. There, dear madam, I expect to see you once more in this land of the dying. If not, ere long, I shall meet you in the land of the living, and thank you, before men and angels, for all favours conferred on me. Tomorrow, God willing, I move again. Before long, my last remove will come; a remove into endless bliss.

In early January Whitefield left Bohemia Manor and traveled south to Virginia. He was struck by what large areas of the colony had no organized Christian work. People traveled forty and fifty miles just to hear him preach—and this in a time when roads were so bad that such a trip would typically take ten hours one way. Seeing such a response to the gospel, Whitefield wished he could spend more time in Virginia. "Had I not been detained so long at the northward," he wrote, "what a wide and effectual door might have been opened. Here, as well as elsewhere, rich and poor flock to hear the everlasting gospel."

Whitefield also wanted to sail from Charleston to the West Indies. Many of those islands had large English-speaking populations, but, as in Virginia, there was not much Christian ministry. Whitefield understood that the potential for a large ministry existed in the West Indies, but that winter of 1755 was not a time for him to go. Obligations at Bethesda called him back to Georgia. Nothing is known of what happened during his travels from Virginia to the orphanage or about what he did while at Bethesda. We do know that something happened during that time period that brought him tremendous heartache. On February 26 he left Bethesda for Charleston, from where he would leave for England. In a letter written from Charleston on March 3, Whitefield alluded to the painful event: "The trials I have met with have brought my old vomitings upon me. My soul has been pierced with many sorrows. But, I believe, all is intended for my good. Amidst all, I am comforted at the present situation of Bethesda."

Consistently, Whitefield indicates that the orphanage in Georgia was a source of happiness for him. In another letter written from Charleston on March 17, he admitted, "Had I wings like a dove, how often would I have fled to Bethesda, since my departure from it! I could almost say that the last few hours I was there, were superior in satisfaction to any hours I ever enjoyed. But I must go about my heavenly Father's business." Ten days later George Whitefield set sail for England. In spite of his ties with the American colonies in general and the Bethesda orphanage in particular, it would be more than eight years before he visited America again.

twelve

When George Whitefield returned to England in May 1755, the forty-year-old man was not prepared for the storm of protests he was about to face. Things began normally enough. He preached throughout London and the surrounding area to large crowds. He reported by letter to the Countess of Huntingdon and other people who supported his work, and he renewed relationships with people he had come to know during his sixteen years of public ministry.

War broke out between France and England, but Whitefield's primary concern at the beginning of the war was the well-being of his friends in America. The colonies became involved in the war because both France and England claimed territory in the New World.

As was typical throughout Whitefield's life, he stuck to an incredibly demanding schedule. On November 1 he wrote from London: "On Thursday evening, I came to town, after having preached about a hundred times, and travelled about eight hundred miles. For more than ten days together, I preached thrice a day. O that I could preach three hundred times!"

Shortly after he wrote that letter he joined the Countess of Huntingdon at her home in Bristol. Although he planned on preaching, his intense schedule caught up with him once again. At the end of November he wrote from Bristol, "For near ten days past, I have preached in pain, occasioned by a sore throat, which I find now is the beginning of a quinsy [an inflammation of the tonsils]. The doctor tells me silence and warmth may cure me; but (if I had my will) heaven is my choice, especially if I can speak no longer for my God on earth. However, painful as the medicine of silence is, I have promised to be very obedient, and, therefore, I have not preached this morning."

Toward the end of the year, George Whitefield returned to London. His throat, although not healed, had recovered to the point that he could once again speak, and he was excited about the prospect of preaching at a new chapel that had been built in Long Acre. Located in London's West End near the theaters, it was accessible to the fashionable members of society to whom Whitefield continued to have an important ministry. At first he preached there twice a week. Hundreds of people had to be turned away because there wasn't enough room for them.

Whitefield was known for his public criticisms of the theater, and because he knew that many in his audiences

at Long Acre had just left one of the many theater performances, he incorporated those ideas into his Long
Acre sermons. "You go to plays!" he said, "and what do
you see there! Why, if you will not tell me, I will tell you
what you see there! When you see the players on the
stage, you see the devil's children grinning at you."[1]

While some performers were tolerant of Whitefield's
criticisms, others worried that he would draw crowds
away from their plays and make a serious dent in the
amount of money they made. Their opposition was fueled
even more by an incorrect rumor that Whitefield had
caused a theater to be torn down.

Some members of the actors' guild took steps to dis-
rupt his services. Soon every sermon he preached was
interrupted by people outside the building ringing bells,
banging drums, and singing rowdy songs. When Whitefield continued to preach and people continued to listen
to him, the hecklers began throwing stones at both
Whitefield and those who supported him. Whitefield
reported stones weighing up to a pound breaking the
chapel windows during services. Fortunately, they did
not cause any serious injuries.

"Drummers, soldiers, and many of the baser sort have
been hired by subscription. A copper furnace, bells,
drums, clappers, marrow bones and cleavers and such like
instruments of reformation have been provided for and
made use of by them, from the moment I have begun
preaching to the end of my sermon," Whitefield wrote.

Early in April 1756 Whitefield received three anony-
mous letters threatening that unless he stopped preaching in Long Acre, he would have "a certain, sudden and
unavoidable stroke." Whitefield had no doubt that some

of his enemies were plotting to kill him.

As the threats and violence continued, people totally removed from the world of theater were swept into the conflict. Some Roman Catholics reacted to a pamphlet Whitefield wrote about the ongoing war between England and France.

Relationships between Protestants and Roman Catholics during the 1700s were terrible. For more than two hundred years, Roman Catholic and Protestant nations had fought wars against each other. England itself had changed back and forth between being officially Catholic or officially Protestant. Each time the approved religion changed, thousands of innocent people were killed. Both sides distrusted each other, and both sides were responsible for the murders of those whose religion differed from theirs.

When war broke out between France and England in 1755, the Church of England had been Protestant for generations. The official French church was Roman Catholic. In supporting Britain's war against France, Whitefield charged Catholic priests in the colonies with inciting Native American tribes to kill English subjects in America, mentioning "shocking accounts of the horrid butcheries and cruel murders committed." He went on to charge Roman Catholic countries with martyring thousands of innocent Protestants.

Many English Roman Catholics were angered to see Catholicism attacked with such inflammatory language, although similar attacks against both Protestants and Catholics were fairly common in those days. English Roman Catholics also felt it was unfair for Whitefield to

147

ignore the number of Roman Catholics who had died at the hands of Protestants.

Bombarded with criticism and abuse from several different directions, George Whitefield realized that he could not continue to preach at Long Acre. But he also believed the threats against his life should not be ignored. So he took several steps. First, he used his aristocratic contacts to bring the matter of the death threats to the attention of King George II. On April 30, 1756, an announcement from the palace about the threatening letters Whitefield had received appeared in the *London Gazette*. In part, it read:

> *His Majesty, for the better discovering and bringing to justice the persons concerned in writing and sending the three letters. . .is pleased to promise his most gracious pardon to any one of them, who shall discover his or her accomplice or accomplices therein, so that he, she or they may be apprehended and convicted thereof.*

While the notice didn't lead to any arrests, it did discourage people from making any more threats or physically attacking Whitefield.

Whitefield also decided to build another chapel in London at Tottenham Court Road. He chose the site because it was close enough to Long Acre so that the people who had been attending those services could still reach it easily. At the same time, it was far enough away from the theater district to discourage the rioters from disrupting his sermons. In November Whitefield held the first meetings in the new facility.

The Tottenham Chapel not only provided an area for services, but like many churches in England, it had vaults beneath the building set apart for burials. Whitefield planned to have himself and his wife buried there, as well as the pastors of the chapel and other significant contributors to the work. But he also saw the chapel as providing one more opportunity to demonstrate the healed relationships between himself and the Wesley brothers.

The headquarters for John Wesley's work was an old cannon factory, which some felt an inappropriate place for someone to be buried. So Whitefield made it known that he wanted the Wesley brothers to be buried at Tottenham Chapel. Always direct in his speech, Whitefield took clear aim at his followers who still held grudges against the Wesleys: "I have prepared a vault in this chapel, where I intend to be buried," he said, "and Messrs. John and Charles Wesley shall also be buried there. We will all lie together. You will not let them enter your chapel while they are alive. They can do you no harm when they are dead."

As usual, Whitefield spent the winter in London with his wife. Not only did he speak about fifteen times a week at Tottenham Chapel and the Tabernacle, but he also oversaw the building of twelve almshouses where many poor widows could live rent-free. He tried to maintain contact with friends in both America and the Georgia orphanage, but because of the war between England and France, it took longer for the ships carrying his letters to cross the Atlantic. Many ships were destroyed by enemy fire before they completed their journeys.

The welfare of the orphanage weighed heavily upon

Whitefield's mind. As a civilian, he couldn't cross the Atlantic and visit Bethesda in person until the war was over. Reports circulated that the Spanish in Florida were preparing to invade Georgia by way of the Atlantic Ocean. Other rumors claimed that the French were encouraging Native Americans to attack Georgia by land. Whitefield found himself in the unusual position of not being able to intervene directly. He was forced to wait for infrequent mail from Georgia and pray about a situation that he knew little about.

Family troubles also landed in George Whitefield's lap. His brother Thomas appeared at Tabernacle House in London, wanting to hide from creditors to whom he owed money because of a failed business. Two nephews, George and James Whitefield, became the responsibility of their uncle.

Perhaps because of his additional obligations in London, George Whitefield didn't begin his journeys in 1757 until late April. After traveling for sixteen days, he arrived in Edinburgh, where he stayed for a month. This was his ninth visit to Scotland, and as he had done in the past, he held open air meetings each morning and evening. From Edinburgh he traveled to Glasgow, where he raised money for relief work among the poor of the city. Then in June, rather than returning to England, Whitefield decided to go to Ireland. He arrived in Dublin in mid-June and continued preaching there for several weeks. Most of his preaching took place in arrangement with the Wesleyan societies scattered throughout the area.

During the war between England and France, Whitefield's habit was to preach about Christ and encourage his audiences to honor King George, "the best of kings," as he described him. On a Sunday morning in July, Whitefield conducted such a service and closed by praying for "the success of the Prussian arms." This prayer referred to Frederick, the king of Prussia, whose military support was helping the English in their battles in Europe. The English saw Frederick as a Protestant hero and celebrated his birthday.

In praying for Frederick and his armies, Whitefield chose to ignore how Roman Catholics in Ireland might react to his support of someone they perceived as an enemy. Whitefield was already well-known for his anti-Catholic statements, and that afternoon an enraged mob, finding Whitefield alone in a field, began stoning the man. Whitefield kept walking, but he was soon covered with blood. A beaver hat he was wearing gave his head some protection initially, but soon something knocked the hat off, and he was hit on the head by several stones. All Whitefield could think of was the story of the stoning of Stephen in Acts 7. He became convinced that, like Stephen, he himself would soon die.

He reached town, found a Methodist minister's house, and managed to stagger to the door. Temporarily, Whitefield had found safety. But the mob surrounded the house, and the minister's wife was terrified that the people would destroy her home. Still, she didn't want to send Whitefield on his way to a certain death. Just at that moment another Methodist preacher with two friends pulled up in front of the house in a coach. Whitefield leaped from the doorway to the vehicle and was carried away to safety, but for the rest of his life he carried a large scar near one of his temples.

In spite of the attack, Whitefield continued to preach in Ireland for another three weeks, but he never returned to that country again. In August he left for London, where he arrived by the end of the month.

Except for a short trip to Plymouth, he spent the rest of the year in London. During the winter of 1757–1758 George Whitefield began to admit to some of his physical limitations. In a letter to Professor Francke of Halle University in Germany, he wrote: "In the Winter I am confined to this metropolis; but to my great mortification, through continual vomiting, want of rest and of appetite, I have been reduced for some time to the short allowance of preaching only once a day except *Sundays,* when I generally preach thrice."

These concessions were only the beginning for Whitefield, now forty-three years old, of learning to deal with physical weakness. As soon as spring arrived he left London, determined to preach through England and Wales. Ignoring past experiences, he forced himself to preach two to three times a day, and after three weeks in Wales, he was so weak that he couldn't even sit up in bed when people came to visit him.

Realizing that this situation couldn't continue, he decided to change his mode of travel. He had already changed from riding horseback to using a two-wheeled chaise. But having declared, "The Welch roads have almost demolished my open, one horse chaise as well as me," he bought a closed, four-wheeled vehicle that made travel much more comfortable. While this change allowed him more rest, he still spent much of the summer of 1758 fighting illnesses of various kinds.

Whitefield was also beginning to understand the restraints placed on him by his obligations to the two churches in London as well as the orphanage. No longer could he spend uninterrupted months as an itinerant preacher. He was frequently called back to London because no one was available to preach at the Tabernacle or the Chapel or because some other administrative crisis had erupted.

One burden was slightly eased. At some point during 1758, Whitefield received a legacy to use however he saw fit. He immediately designated it for the orphanage, relieving some of the constant financial stress that institution faced.

But personal losses added to Whitefield's load. That summer he learned of the death of Jonathan Edwards in New Jersey. And after Whitefield's return to London for the winter, he learned of the serious illness of his good friend James Hervey. In a letter to Hervey written on December 19, 1758, Whitefield stated: "And is my dear friend indeed about to take his last flight? I dare not wish your return into this vale of tears. But our prayers are continually ascending to the Father of our spirits that you may die in the embraces of a never-failing Jesus, and in all the fulness of an exalted faith. O when will my time come! I groan in this tabernacle, being burdened, and long to be clothed with my house from heaven." On Christmas Day, Hervey died.

The Seven Years' War continued unabated, even though the death of King George II in 1760 led to Britain crowning a new king. George III was the grandson of George II and shared his grandfather's commitment to defeating France.

Because of the political situation, Whitefield continued to funnel what energies he had into ministry on the British Isles. During the summer of 1760, a new play was produced in London. "The Minor," written by Samuel Foote, was an obvious parody of Methodists in general and George Whitefield in particular. The character of Dr. Squintum was unmistakably Foote's depiction of Whitefield, and it drew attention to Whitefield's eye that had been damaged from measles when he was a child. The play crudely suggested inappropriate relationships between Whitefield and various women and was called blasphemous by many leaders of English society. However, it also drew large crowds and was a financial success.

Whitefield's only known response to the play appeared in a letter in which he wrote: "I am now mimicked and burlesqued upon the public stage. All hail such contempt!" But the stress of hearing children sing nasty songs about Dr. Squintum and of being on the receiving end of coarse jokes further weakened his health. He caught a severe cold in November, and by the beginning of 1761, he was a bedridden invalid, seldom able to preach.

For months Whitefield's health did not improve, and by April his friends thought him close to death. Over the next year he sought the advice of several physicians. When he followed their instructions, his health improved. But each time he began feeling better, he began preaching again and his illnesses would return. By the spring of 1762, he was even weaker than he had been the year before.

That June he finally took a ship to Rotterdam. His time in Holland improved his health significantly, and after he returned to England, that improvement continued. Once again he felt able to preach, but whenever he pushed his body to do more than it was able, he again fell ill. Even as stubborn a man as George Whitefield was beginning to understand that he needed to delegate some of his responsibilities. In a letter to Robert Keen written that fall, he said, "Once a day preaching, I can bear well; more hurts me. What shall I do with the Chapel and Tabernacle? Lord Jesus, be thou my guide and helper! He will! He will!"

Late in 1762 the Seven Years' War between England and France ended. Immediately Whitefield made plans to leave as soon as possible for America. He delegated the management of the Tabernacle and the Chapel to three of his trusted friends: Robert Keen, Charles Hardy, and Mr. Beckman. "O that the Lord may incline your heart[s] to accept this trust!" he told them. "It will take off this ponderous load that oppresses me much."

George Whitefield was anxious to see his friends in the American colonies. It had been almost eight years since he had last crossed the Atlantic, and finally he could see his way clear to leave England for the New World.

thirteen

George Whitefield made plans to sail for America from Scotland in the middle of April 1763 on board the *Jenny*. The ship offered unusually comfortable accommodations and should have provided him with an easy voyage and improved health. But when the *Jenny* was ready to sail, Whitefield was too ill to get on board. Instead he stayed in Scotland until June, dogged by illness and fatigue.

John Wesley visited him in May and afterward wrote, "At Edinburgh, I had the satisfaction of spending a little time with Mr. Whitefield. Humanly speaking, he is worn out; but we have to do with Him who hath all power in heaven and earth."

In spite of his sickness, Whitefield insisted on continuing to preach. Not surprisingly, by June he was seriously ill. One newspaper reported that Whitefield would be unable to travel. However, Whitefield recovered enough to be able to set sail on the *Fanny,* bound for Rappahanock, Virginia, on June 4, 1763.

This Atlantic crossing was unusually long, lasting the better part of three months. While at first, sailing was smooth and Whitefield enjoyed breathing the cool, moist ocean breezes, the weather changed. Storms and rough seas battered the ship. Whitefield described the last six weeks of the trip as "very trying to my shattered bark." He assessed his physical condition with these words: "A few exertions, like the last struggles of a dying man, or glimmering flashes of a taper just burning out, [are] all that can be expected from me." These were grim words indeed from a man who was not yet fifty years old and who saw many of his contemporaries live into their seventies and eighties.

To the great relief of all on board, the ship at last reached Virginia on August 24. News of Whitefield's arrival spread quickly. He longed to visit Bethesda, the orphanage in Georgia, but recognizing that summer heat in the southern colonies would not improve his health, he instead headed for Philadelphia.

Whitefield's longtime friend Ben Franklin was away from the city when he arrived. Franklin was inspecting the post offices throughout the colonies, a journey that covered roughly eighteen hundred miles and took more than seven months. But many other past associates were eager to greet the minister they had not seen for more than eight years.

Although they had been told of Whitefield's illnesses, many of the people must have been shocked at the change in his appearance. When they had last seen him, Whitefield was young, slender, and full of energy. Now he was obviously exhausted, moved slowly, and had gained weight. While they expressed hopes of hearing Whitefield speak twice a day as he had in the past, people in Philadelphia had to be satisfied with two sermons a week. The response to the English minister, however, was still affectionate. Hundreds flocked to hear him speak, as if thinking this might be their last opportunity. It was obvious that the Whitefield they had known as an energetic young man was now quite ill.

Whitefield was understandably frustrated to be so close to Georgia yet still unable to visit Bethesda. And while doctors' warnings about the ill effects of the southern climate were part of the reason he stayed away, he was also aware that a journey to Georgia was unsafe for anyone during the fall of 1763. While the Seven Years' War between France and England had ended, conflict between the French and British colonists continued, as did periodic attacks by some Native Americans.

So he spent September, October, and most of November in Philadelphia. In spite of his frustrations over what he couldn't do, Whitefield found some things to be thankful for. In a letter he wrote to a friend on October 21, he said, "Here are some young bright witnesses rising up in the church. Perhaps I have already conversed with forty new-creature ministers of various denominations. Sixteen hopeful students. . .were converted at New Jersey College [now Princeton University] last year."

Near the end of November, Whitefield and his traveling companion, James Habersham, headed north to New York. They stopped at both New Jersey College and Elizabeth Town, New Jersey, on their way. Whitefield's health was slowly improving, and he noted in a letter written on December 1 that "thrice a week is as often as I can preach." Stubborn as the minister was, he understood that it would be foolhardy, on the basis of such slim improvement, to venture all the way to Georgia. "Today, I. . .have thoughts of returning with Mr. Habersham to Georgia, but am fearful of relapsing by such a fatiguing journey," he wrote in the same letter.

Within a week Whitefield had reached a decision about the orphanage. He had experienced more than enough of learning about it and managing it by letter. Instead, he sent James Habersham to visit Bethesda in person and deal with financial issues and other management problems that needed direct intervention. "What a mortification it is to me not to accompany my dear Mr. Habersham to Bethesda," he wrote to people at the orphanage. "Assure yourselves, I shall come as soon as possible. Meanwhile, I have desired Mr. Habersham to assist in supervising and settling the accounts, and to give his advice respecting the house, plantation, etc."

Whitefield spent the remainder of the year in New York. When not resting or preaching, he visited with people who wanted to discuss the gospel and wrote letters to friends both in the colonies and back in England. The day after Christmas he sent a note to his old friend Charles Wesley, reporting how encouraged he was by the openness of the people and the number of young "new creature" ministers he was meeting. News traveling as slowly as it did, Whitefield didn't want to assume anything about the well-being of the Wesley family, so he closed his letter with these words: "I hope your brother lives and prospers. Remember me to your dear yoke-fellow, and all enquiring friends; and assure yourselves of not being forgotten in the poor addresses of, my dear friend, Yours in Jesus, George Whitefield."

As 1764 began Whitefield was still in New York, expressing a strong desire to be in Georgia. But a hope that the colder northern climate would improve his health led him instead to New England.

Before he left New York, the *Boston Gazette* printed a report of the work he had done during his seven weeks in New York City. Specifically, it mentioned two charity sermons Whitefield preached: "One on the occasion of the annual collection for the poor, when double the sum was collected than ever was upon the like occasion; the other for the benefit of Mr. Wheelock's Indian School, at Lebanon, in New England, for which he collected (notwithstanding the prejudices of many people against the Indians) the sum of £120." However his health may have deteriorated over the years, George Whitefield had lost none of his persuasive powers when speaking on a subject about which he felt passionately.

And Whitefield's health was continuing to improve. As he headed for Boston, he again began trying to preach once a day. Apparently the experiment was not a success, because after a week in Boston he wrote, "Twice a week is as often as I can with comfort ascend my throne [pulpit]."

Yet wherever Whitefield went in Boston, he was warmly greeted. Four years earlier the city had experienced a devastating fire. Nearly four hundred homes were destroyed. When he learned of the disaster, Whitefield had turned to the people in his London churches and raised money which he then sent to the city's officials. Now that he was visiting the city in person, the city felt it only appropriate to show some sign of gratitude.

A newspaper account, dated February 20, describes that "Monday last, at a very general meeting of the free-holders and other inhabitants of this town, it was voted unanimously that the thanks of the town be given to the Rev. Mr. George Whitefield, for his charitable care and pains in collecting a considerable sum of money in Great Britain, for the benefit of the distressed sufferers by the great fire in Boston, 1760. And a respectable committee was appointed to wait on Mr. Whitefield, to inform him of the vote, and present him with a copy thereof."

In March Whitefield decided to leave Boston for more northern settlements, hoping to travel as far as Canada. He had two reasons for this trip. As always, he thrived on meeting new people and preaching wherever he could. But he also learned that smallpox was expected in Boston and wanted to avoid exposure to the disease—a wise precaution given the general state of his health.

During his time both in Boston and in the surrounding area, he raised funds for two other causes. Through letters to wealthy friends in England and other contacts, he was able to make a significant donation to Harvard College (as it was then called) to help replace books lost in a library fire after the Boston fire in 1760. He also continued to raise money for Wheelock's Indian School in Lebanon, Connecticut.

The school, founded by the Reverend Eleazar Wheelock, was originally intended for white boys. But in 1743 a young Mohegan Indian named Samson Occum became a student at the school. Samson did so well in his studies that Reverend Wheelock was struck by the idea of training more Indian boys so that they could become missionaries to their own people. Soon he had twenty Native American boys studying at his school.

Whitefield saw the value of training members of the various Native American tribes to spread the gospel among their people. He not only raised funds for Wheelock's New England school, but he also sent letters to some of his more influential and wealthy friends in England. Lord Dartmouth, in particular, was struck by this outreach and became an ardent supporter. A few years later Samson Occum traveled to England to raise money, and he met with Dartmouth. Largely because of that trip, sufficient funds were raised to move the school to New Hampshire on donated land, where it would be closer to the Native Americans. Shortly afterward a college was built in the same location and named Dartmouth in tribute to Lord Dartmouth's support.

As Whitefield slowly made his way toward Portsmouth, New Hampshire, he also maintained contact with the two churches in London. The reports he received from the three trustees greatly encouraged him. But once again, he pushed his body too hard. When he reached Portsmouth in the spring of 1764, he suffered a serious relapse. For days he could not get out of bed, and he was forced to admit that he wouldn't be able to travel to Canada. Instead, he decided that once he was in somewhat better health, he would slowly make his way to Georgia and the orphanage.

His first stop was in Boston, where he stayed for a week or two. But residents of the city were so intent on seeing more of George Whitefield that they literally followed him out of the city and forced him to turn back. After about eight more weeks in Boston, he continued toward New York, stopping first at New Haven College in Connecticut, which is now Yale University. During earlier trips to the colonies, the college's president, Mr. Clapp, had disagreed strongly with Whitefield on many issues and seemed generally hostile toward the English minister. But by 1764 much of the controversy of the Great Awakening had dissipated, and Mr. Clapp was much friendlier toward his guest. When Whitefield finished preaching to the students, Mr. Clapp even asked him to "give them one more quarter of an hour's exhortation."

By summer Whitefield had reached New York City. He not only preached in various churches throughout the city, but he also took short trips to Long Island where he preached outside. Most people arrived at these meetings on foot, but he reported that he would also see more than one hundred carriages at each of these sermons.

Whitefield was determined to reach the orphanage sometime in 1764, but as the summer stretched on, everyone advised him not to head farther south than New York until September. Hot as it was in that northern city, it was even worse to the south. Grudgingly, he took their advice, and his health gradually improved.

By the middle of September Whitefield had left New York and reached Philadelphia, with hopes of getting to Georgia before Christmas. In Philadelphia he was quickly asked to preach at the commencement of the new term at the College of Philadelphia. On September 21 he wrote a letter to Robert Keen, one of the trustees of the two churches in London. In it he commented, "I have only preached twice here, but the influence was deep. I am better in health than I have been these three years."

A few days later he also wrote to Charles Wesley, mentioning that he had just received a letter Wesley had written eight months earlier. Describing the spiritual mood of the colonies, he wrote: "Had strength permitted, I might have preached to thousands and thousands thrice every day. Zealous ministers are not so rare in this new world as in other parts. Here is room for a hundred itinerants. Lord Jesus, send by whom Thou wilt send!" These and other letters from Whitefield contributed to the Wesley brothers sending more Methodist ministers to the American colonies over the next several years.

Around October 21 George Whitefield left Philadelphia, heading toward Virginia. From there he traveled to North and South Carolina. At every stop he visited with "New Lights," a name given to evangelical preachers and their converts. These groups were similar to the Methodists in England, and he thoroughly enjoyed spending time with such eager listeners.

Sometime in early December Whitefield finally reached Georgia. It had been almost ten years since he had last set foot in Bethesda, and he immediately took action to enlarge the ministry at the orphanage. One of his ideas was to ask the governor and council of the colony to donate two thousand acres of land so that Whitefield could build a college. In correspondence to these leaders, he pointed out that no institution of higher learning existed south of Virginia. He also reminded them of all that the orphanage had contributed to Georgia during its early days as a colony. Because of the work at Bethesda, many poor people had been able to stay in Georgia when otherwise they would have been forced to leave, and each developing colony needed all the able-bodied colonists it could find.

Whitefield's efforts were helped by the fact that his old friend James Habersham, whom Whitefield had sent to Bethesda a year earlier to act as superintendent, was now the president of Georgia's council. The governor and council agreed to recommend that the Privy Council in London approve Whitefield's request, but Whitefield thought it would be wise to press his case with the members of the Privy Council in person. So he planned on returning to England as soon as possible.

North Atlantic crossings were notoriously treacherous during the winter, so Whitefield remained at Bethesda until February 1765. He enjoyed the relative quiet at the orphanage and was able to focus on managing its needs rather than simultaneously carrying the responsibilities of itinerant preaching, running the two churches in London, raising funds for various charitable causes, and taking care of the orphanage. He relaxed throughout his stay in Georgia and continued corresponding with several friends, including Benjamin Franklin, who was traveling throughout the northern colonies.

The orphanage also successfully underwent an audit of its finances, and as Whitefield prepared to leave, he was satisfied that all debts had been paid off, and that Bethesda had some cash available in addition to crops and lumber from the preceding year. Smallpox had taken the lives of six slaves and four orphans, but Whitefield was pleased that in twenty-four years of existence, only four other children had died. This was a remarkable record, given the number of childhood diseases at the time for which there was no effective treatment and the fact that these illnesses would spread much more quickly in an institutional environment such as an orphanage.

As a result of his winter's rest, Whitefield's health improved so much that he decided to postpone leaving for England in the spring. Instead, he once again began an itinerant evangelistic tour of the southern colonies and followed the warm spring weather to the north.

By May Whitefield was in Delaware, where he composed a letter to Robert Keen, one of the trustees at the London churches. Because of the death of Mr. Beckman, only two trustees remained, but George Whitefield was beginning to realize that their services would continue to be needed after he returned to England. His spring travels had erased much of his improved health. As he wrote to Keen: "I have no manner of prospect of being able to serve the tabernacle and chapel. I cannot preach once now, without being quite exhausted. How then shall I bear the cares of both those places? But I must beg you and dear Mr H[ard]y to continue as trustees when I am present, as well as in my absence. I wish that a ship was ready now, perhaps I may yet sail from New York."

And on June 9 Whitefield did set sail from New York Harbor. For once, the sea passage was smooth, and the ship arrived in England on July 7, making the journey in only twenty-eight days. Feeling ill and dreading the thought of taking up his responsibilities in London, he left the ship in Falmouth, along England's southern coast. Falmouth was the first English port his ship stopped at, and by landing there, Whitefield would take longer than usual to reach London. In a letter to Robert Keen, he wrote: "I am very

166

low in body, and as yet undetermined what to do. Perhaps on the whole it may be best to come on leisurely, to see if my spirits can be a little recruited. . . . Had I bodily strength, you would find me coming upon you unawares; but that fails me much. I must have a little rest, or I shall be able to do nothing at all."

His body might have been at the breaking point, but no one understood better than George Whitefield the expectations he would face once his arrival in England became public knowledge.

fourteen

George Whitefield made his way to London and arrived by the first part of August 1765. Still in poor health, he felt obligated to do what he could for the Tabernacle and Chapel. One of the tasks he took up was to make sure speakers were scheduled for all the services held at the two churches. He wrote to ministers he knew throughout England, asking them to speak in London.

In a letter written on September 20 to one of those men, Andrew Kinsman, Whitefield mentioned that his wife, Elizabeth, had returned to London the night before. Elizabeth Whitefield's body had never recovered from her miscarriages and illnesses. She typically spent the summer months in the country and returned to the Whitefield home in London for the winter. Her husband's letter alluded to her health problems: "She indulges this morning, being weary; but, I take it for granted, that, you and I rise at five."

In spite of his pronouncements about getting up early, Whitefield still suffered from respiratory problems, and the smoky air of London most likely aggravated his underlying problems. In the same letter to Kinsman, Whitefield noted, "I shall never breathe as I would, till I breathe in heaven."

His return to England also placed Whitefield under obligation to the Countess of Huntingdon once again. For twenty-five years she had visited Bath and used that fashionable city as a place for evangelism to the aristocracy. Having already built chapels at her homes in Brighton and Bristol, she had just completed a third chapel at her home in Bath. She invited six clergy, including Whitefield, to the opening of the chapel, which was held on October 6.

George Whitefield set out to make the more than one-hundred-mile journey on October 1. He preached at the service held on the morning of October 6, and wrote the next day to Robert Keen that he was scheduled to preach again on Tuesday night and had hopes of leaving for London on Wednesday. Poor health and bad weather, however, probably conspired to keep Whitefield in London for the rest of the year.

On October 28 he had breakfast with Charles Wesley, who observed later that his friend was "an old, old man, fairly worn out in his Master's service, though he has hardly seen fifty years." At that same time, Whitefield described himself in a letter to Bethesda as "better than I was last year."

The conflict between the two descriptions may reflect that Wesley was able to be more objective

169

because he had not seen his friend for more than two years. Also, after so many years of illness, Whitefield may simply have become used to feeling badly and not noticed that what he considered good days, other people viewed as marginal at best.

While in London, Whitefield did what he could to promote the idea of founding a college in the Georgia Colony. The governor and council of Georgia had already forwarded Whitefield's request to the Privy Council in England, and Lord Dartmouth was a prominent supporter of the idea. But because religious issues were involved— such as whether the college would adhere to the Church of England or be nondenominational—the matter was referred to the Archbishop of Canterbury, Dr. Thomas Secker. Impatient that no decision had been made, during the winter of 1765–1766, Whitefield appealed directly to King George III. The king also referred the matter to the Archbishop of Canterbury, so Whitefield was forced to continue waiting.

Not one to sit idly, Whitefield turned his energies toward helping John Wesley. While Whitefield had been in America for two years, conflict over the doctrine of perfection had threatened to split the Wesley Societies permanently. The conflict began shortly before Whitefield's departure for America when one of John Wesley's early assistants, George Bell, and other members of the societies began teaching that they were "as holy as the angels" and "incapable of ever sinning again."

John Wesley did not take as extreme a position and publicly disagreed with them. They responded by claiming that they were simply teaching what John Wesley himself had taught them and that Wesley was rejecting his own teachings.

To further complicate matters, Wesley believed that Thomas Maxfield, who had worked with him for more than twenty years, was siding with George Bell. Maxfield vehemently denied this charge, but Wesley refused to change his mind. As a result, Maxfield left Wesley and began his own chapel in London. Hundreds of Wesley's followers left with Maxfield.

By the time Whitefield returned to England, bad feelings still existed between George Bell and John Wesley. During that winter Whitefield sought out George Bell, and as a result, Bell's attitude toward Wesley changed. On January 3, 1766, John Wesley wrote: "Mr. Bell called upon me, now calm, and in his right mind. God has repressed his furious, bitter zeal, by means of Mr. Whitefield."

About a month later Samson Occum, the Mohegan Indian who was associated with Mr. Wheelock's Indian school in America, arrived in England with the Reverend Whitaker. For a year and a half, the duo traveled throughout Great Britain, preaching and presenting the needs of Native Americans. Occum was the first Native American to preach in England, and crowds gathered wherever he spoke. Shortly after Occum arrived, Whitefield arranged for him to preach at Tottenham Court Chapel in London and did whatever he could to help make Occum and Whitaker's travels succeed.

Not all was good news that year. George Whitefield's brother James died at the Bath home of the Countess of Huntingdon, and responsibilities for the two London churches weighed heavily on George Whitefield's mind.

171

At the first sign of spring, he was ready to travel to Bath and Bristol.

This trip was short, and by April Whitefield was back in London, where he stayed for two months. Health continued to curtail his activities. In a letter to the Reverend John Gillies of Glasgow, Whitefield wrote, "Not want of love, but of leisure and better health, has prevented you hearing from me more frequently. I find I cannot do as I have done." In another letter from that same period he wrote, "Though at present I am almost in a breathless state, by preaching last night, yet I hope to be strengthened to give the holy sacrament at seven next Sunday morning; and, if able, to preach afterwards at ten." At fifty-one years of age, George Whitefield struggled to be able to preach only one-tenth as often as he had when he was in his twenties.

In June Whitefield once again set out for Bath and Bristol, still complaining of his "feverish heat." While testing the curative powers of the waters in Bath, he also managed to preach every morning at six o'clock. When he returned to London in August, he met several times with John and Charles Wesley. The aim of these meetings was to create a closer working relationship among the three of them and the Countess of Huntingdon. One outcome of these meetings was that the Wesleys were allowed to preach in the three chapels owned by the countess. Charles Wesley called the group a "quadruple alliance," and the joint work continued until Whitefield's death.

While Whitefield was achieving success in many of his ministry relationships, his physical ailments continued to frustrate him. In a September 1 letter from London, he wrote, "Besides, bodily weakness prevents my writing as formerly." In another letter written on September 25, he apologized: "I am sorry your letter has been so long unanswered; but bodily weakness, and a multiplicity of correspondents, at home and abroad, must be pleaded as excuses. . . . Had I wings, I would gladly fly from pole to pole; but they are clipped by the feeble labours of thirty years. Twice or thrice a week, I am permitted to ascend my gospel-throne [pulpit]. Pray that the last glimmering of an expiring taper may be blessed to the guiding of many wandering souls to the Lamb of God."

Unlike other years, it did not seem to matter where Whitefield lived. His health did not improve. In November he wrote to Robert Keen from Bath: "I have been low ever since my coming here. The Bath air, I believe, will never agree with me long. However, if good is done, all will be well." When he arrived at Bristol later in the month, he wrote, "I am just come here, weary, but am going to speak a few words."

Not only was Whitefield undergoing physical attacks, but he also faced more attacks in print. Pamphlets were sold, accusing him of lacking financial integrity ("Behold here one of the *righteous* over-much—yet nought doth he give away in charity!"); being unfaithful to God ("He knows his *Master's* realm so well,/His sermons are a *map* of hell"); and indulging in hypocrisy ("With *one* eye he looks up to heaven, to make his congregation think he is *devout*, that's his *spiritual* eye; and with the other eye he looks down to see what he can get, and that's his *carnal* eye").

As had become his habit, Whitefield ignored such writings and focused on his ministry. He began 1767 by

173

writing a preface to the third edition of the works of John Bunyan. He also began to feel better, although not well. With more strength than he had enjoyed in months, George Whitefield once again started speaking throughout Great Britain. Letters written from April through June show him in both England and Wales. While he still tired easily, the sight of hundreds of people coming to hear him preach the gospel energized George Whitefield like nothing else.

The summer found Whitefield once again in London, taking care of business for the two churches, but in September he left for a tour of northern England. On September 28, writing from Thirsk, he reported: "My body feels much fatigue in travelling; comforts in the soul over-balance. Every stage more and more convinces me that old methodism is the thing."

What did he mean by "old methodism"? For many years both George Whitefield and John Wesley complained that the younger men coming up through the ranks of Methodism did not have the same level of commitment as those who came earlier. They were not willing to go through the same kinds of suffering that the founders of the movement had experienced. As Whitefield declared in a sermon, "There are few who like to go out into the fields. Broken heads and dead cats are no longer the ornaments of a Methodist. These honorable badges are now no more. . . . Ye Methodists of many years standing, shew the young ones, who have not the cross to bear, as we once had, what ancient Methodism was."

One of the reasons for this change, of course, was that Methodism was becoming more acceptable. Whitefield himself, though he might be reluctant to admit it, was no longer the lightning rod for controversy that he had been in earlier years. And as every movement ages, it faces new challenges that may not be as vivid, but are just as essential for survival. Many of the younger workers in Methodism chose to work in one parish rather than be involved in itinerant ministry. Through the long-lasting relationships they developed with parishioners, these ministers discipled the next generation of Methodists.

Whitefield did find two younger men whose approach to the ministry he thoroughly endorsed. They became important assistants to him during his last years. The first was Torial Joss, a former sea captain. Joss's early life was far from easy. His father died and his mother neglected him, so he went to sea while quite young. The ship in which he sailed was captured by the French, and he spent years as a prisoner of war. All this happened before he reached his fifteenth birthday.

Released by the French, Joss returned to Scotland, where he was impressed and put aboard a man-of-war. He managed to escape and apprenticed himself to the captain of a small ship that worked along the coast of Scotland and England. While on shore one day, Joss overheard a religious conversation. The impact of those words, along with the writings of John Bunyan, convinced him to become a Christian. He joined a Wesley Society when he was eighteen years old, began preaching in public during his free time, and was encouraged by Wesley himself to continue preaching.

As soon as Joss completed his apprenticeship, he was appointed first mate of his master's ship. He made a habit of preaching whenever the ship came into port. At one stop, a press gang dragged him through the streets and put him on a ship, where he was held prisoner for seven weeks. Upon his release, he was made a captain of a ship. He held regular worship services for his crew. Word of this captain/preacher reached Whitefield, who learned that Torial Joss was headed for London. Much to Joss's surprise, when he arrived on the Thames River, he learned that Whitefield had scheduled him to preach at the Tabernacle.

George Whitefield was so impressed by Joss's sermon that he urged him to give up his captaincy and become a full-time preacher. Joss did and became one of Whitefield's assistants.

Whitefield's other young assistant was an army officer, Captain Scott. Scott commanded a regiment during the Seven Years' War. The carnage he witnessed in battle moved him greatly. After the war he returned to England. While hunting with some friends, a storm struck. Captain Scott sought shelter in a farmer's cottage. There, for the first time, he heard the gospel. The farmer then invited him to go to the nearby village church.

Captain Scott went, and his life was transformed. He immediately began sharing the gospel with his soldiers. Many Christians encouraged him to begin preaching. George Whitefield invited him to be involved with the Tabernacle. Captain Scott resigned his army commission and entered the ministry. Most of his work was done in connection with both the Tabernacle and the Chapel in London.

Meanwhile, George Whitefield continued to make time for correspondence. In early 1768 he exchanged letters with his old friend, Benjamin Franklin, who was staying in London. Franklin shared his concerns about the growing tensions in Boston:

I am under continued apprehensions that we may have bad news from America. The sending of soldiers to Boston always appeared to me a dangerous step [referring to increased presence of British soldiers after passage of the Stamp Act and the Quartering Act]; they could do no good, they might occasion mischief. When I consider the warm resentment of a people who think themselves injured and oppressed, and the common insolence of the soldiery who are taught to consider that people as in rebellion, I cannot but fear the consequences of bringing them together. It seems like setting up a smith's forge in a magazine of gunpowder. I see with you that our affairs are not well managed by our rulers here below; I wish I could believe with you, that they are well attended to by those above; I rather suspect, from certain circumstances, that though the general government of the universe is well administered, our particular little affairs are perhaps below notice, and left to take the chance of human prudence or imprudence, as either may happen to be uppermost. It is, however, an uncomfortable thought, and I leave it.

Whitefield, not surprisingly, disagreed with his friend's assessment. He wrote on the pages of the letter, *"Uncomfortable* indeed! And, blessed be God, *unscriptural;* for we are full assured that 'the Lord reigneth,' and are directed to cast *all* our care on Him, because He careth for us."

During this time Whitefield was receiving updates on the progress of Lady Huntingdon's latest plan. She was renovating the ruins of an old castle in Trevecca, Wales, intending to use it as a school for ministers. Her idea was to have young men who were dedicated to God's service stay at the school for three years, during which they would receive free education, room and board, and a suit of clothes each year. Graduates would be able to seek ordination either from the Church of England or from the Methodists.

Whitefield had great hopes for this school. As he spent the spring and summer of 1768 traveling through England and making his fifteenth (and last) trip to Scotland, he again and again sensed the pressing need for more ministers. Much of the antagonism toward Whitefield in Scotland had disappeared. "I am here only in danger of being hugged to death," he wrote.

Toward the end of July Whitefield headed back toward England. His wife Elizabeth, because of her frail health, had remained in London during her husband's travels. Right after he reached home, she was struck by a fever from which she never recovered. On August 9 she died. George Whitefield preached her funeral sermon five days later.

In it, he gave an example of how her private words of encouragement had kept him going in the face of adversity. "Do you remember my preaching in those fields by the old stump of a tree?" he asked. "The multitude was great, and many were disposed to be riotous. At first I addressed them firmly; but when a desperate gang drew near, with the most ferocious and horrid imprecations and menaces, my courage began to fail. My wife was then standing behind me, as I stood on the table. I think I hear her now. She pulled my gown, and, looking up, said, 'George, play the man for your God.' My confidence returned. I spoke to the multitude with boldness and affection. They became still, and many were deeply affected."

George Whitefield was not about to let his wife's death keep him from his ministry. Two days after her funeral, he wrote to Torial Joss, "Let us work whilst it is day. The late unexpected breach is a fresh proof that the night soon cometh, when no man can work. . . . Sweet bereavements, when God Himself fills up the chasm! Through mercy I find it so."

On August 24, less than two weeks after Elizabeth's funeral, George Whitefield preached at the opening of the college at Trevecca, Wales, which the Countess of Huntingdon had been building. Then he hurried back to London where the extreme pressure he'd placed on himself to keep going no matter what finally caught up with him. His health failed and he was once again an invalid.

During the next year, Whitefield experienced a pattern of improving health, followed by intense activity, followed by failing health. He also felt a continuing concern about the orphanage in Georgia and other works in the American colonies. In September 1769 George Whitefield was ready to sail for America once again. This would be his seventh trip to the colonies. While his friends did not know it at the time, Whitefield would never again set foot in England.

fifteen

When fifty-four-year-old George Whitefield stepped on board the *Friendship* on September 4, 1769, he was looking forward to great things. By this time a seasoned seafarer, he inspected his quarters and was pleasantly surprised. "I am comforted on every side," he reported in a letter to friends. "Fine accommodations. A civil captain and passengers. All willing to attend on divine worship. Praise the Lord, O my soul!"

A combination of unfavorable winds and bad storms kept the ship close to England for more than three weeks. On September 5 the travelers encountered a storm so bad that it completely wrecked another ship in the area. The *Friendship* sailed back into port for repairs before heading out again.

While he waited, Whitefield wrote a number of letters, including one to John Wesley. Whitefield was obviously remembering his experiences over the past three decades. "What hath God wrought *for* us, *in* us, *by* us!" he wrote. "I sailed out of these Downs almost thirty-three years ago. O the height, the depth, the length, the breadth of Thy love, O God! Surely it passeth knowledge. . . . I am glad to hear that you had such a Pentecost season at the College [Trevecca, Wales]. One would hope that these are earnests of good things to come, and that our Lord will not remove His candlestick from among us. Duty is ours. Future things belong to Him, who always did, and always will, order all things well."

In the past, Whitefield had encouraged Wesley to send young preachers to the American colonies. Remarkably, just as George Whitefield was sailing to the colonies for the last time, two young men were leaving on another ship to be missionaries in America. They were students of Wesley and would found the first of many Wesleyan societies across the American colonies. Their influence in America would continue to grow, as six years later the colonies declared their independence from England.

On Tuesday, September 19, the *Friendship* tried to leave England once again. At first the weather looked calm with favorable light winds. Many other ships that had been waiting also left shore. But the good weather did not last. A storm arose and violent gales tossed the ship for several days. Fearing for his ship's safety, the captain turned back. He was not alone.

Altogether, it took the ship the better part of three months to complete its journey. During that time, Whitefield wrote letters and sermons, read, and preached to the passengers and crew whenever the weather would permit. When the *Friendship* landed in Charleston, South Carolina, on November 30, 1769, Whitefield's health had improved, but he was far from well. He couldn't resist the opportunity to speak to the crowds who longed to hear him in the port city. For ten days Whitefield preached to large groups. Finally, on December 10, Mr. Wright, the manager at Bethesda, started George Whitefield on his way to the orphanage. They traveled by water because the roads were impassable.

As had always been the case, George Whitefield was able to relax at Bethesda. And he was excited to find out what good shape the orphanage was in. Workers had started building the college, and Whitefield was gratified to see this thirty-year-old dream finally taking shape.

In January 1770 he wrote a letter to Charles Wesley, describing progress at Bethesda. "All admire the goodness, strength, and beauty of the late improvements. In a few months, the intended plan, I hope, will be completed, and a solid, lasting foundation laid for the support and education of many as yet unborn."

Whitefield had decided to withdraw his application for a college charter from the English government. Instead, he applied to the governor and council of Georgia. Savannah, where the council met, was only ten miles away from Bethesda, so Whitefield invited the men to visit the orphanage and see for themselves the work that was taking place. The men agreed, and the visit took place in late January. It featured a sermon from Whitefield and a large meal, as well as a tour of the grounds.

George Whitefield had every reason to believe that his request for a charter would be granted. For one thing, Bethesda was in excellent financial shape. A fairly substantial legacy had been left by a supporter in Scotland.

That money paid off all Bethesda's debts and left it with a large operating fund. Almost five thousand acres were owned free and clear for the orphanage and college. And Whitefield had put considerable thought into how the institution would be run.

With his charter application he also submitted a list of rules by which the college would be operated. These covered everything from a daily schedule to which divinity books would be read. They included the prohibition of cards, dice, and gaming, as well as instructions for good behavior. Students were to provide their own furniture and mattresses. And no one could travel to Savannah without permission.

By spring Whitefield was reasonably certain that a charter would be granted. Although he was not in good health, the warmer weather brought a desire to return to his itinerant preaching. On April 24, 1770, he set out by coastal vessel toward the northern colonies. His first stop was Philadelphia, where he arrived on Sunday, May 6.

"I have my old plan in view," he wrote to a friend. "To travel in these northern parts all summer, and return late in the fall to Georgia. Through infinite mercy, I continue in good health, and am more and more in love with a pilgrim life."

As was usually the case, Whitefield's perception of his health didn't match reality. His body was worn out. But Whitefield continued to push himself. While in Philadelphia, he spoke twice on Sunday as well as on three or four days during the rest of the week. Crowds of people flocked to hear him preach, perhaps realizing it would be their last opportunity.

In early June he traveled 150 miles in the Philadelphia area, preaching every day. "So many new, as well as old, doors are open," he wrote, "that I know not which way to turn myself. However, at present I am bound for New York, and so on further northward."

Using New York City as a base of operations, Whitefield traveled throughout upstate New York. In a letter dated July 29, he recounted arriving at a place where a horse-stealer was about to be executed. Thousands had come to hear Whitefield speak, and the local sheriff allowed the thief to listen to the sermon before he was executed. Whitefield walked with the thief to the gallows and was struck by how softened the man's heart had become. "I went up with him into the cart," he wrote. "He gave a short exhortation. I then stood upon the coffin; added, I trust, a word in season; prayed; gave the blessing; and took my leave. I hope effectual good was done to the hearers and spectators."

During this trip George Whitefield also experienced one of those rare times when someone questioned his teachings to his face. He dined one day with a group of ministers at the home of a friend, the Reverend William Tennent. As he so often did, Whitefield talked about his joy at the thought of soon dying and going to heaven. He asked the others if they did not also feel such joy. Most of them readily agreed, but Tennent was silent. "Brother Tennent," said Whitefield, "you are the oldest man among us. Do you not rejoice that your being called home is so near at hand?"

"I have no wish about it," answered his host. Whitefield refused to drop the issue, so Tennent replied,

"No, sir, it is no pleasure to me at all; and, if you knew your duty, it would be none to you. I have nothing to do with death. My business is to live as *long* as I can, and as *well* as I can."

Whitefield refused to give up. He asked Tennent if he would choose to die if he could. "Sir," answered Tennent, "I have no choice about it. I am God's servant, and have engaged to do His business as long as He pleases to continue me therein." For once, Whitefield was silenced.

The wise words of Whitefield's friend did nothing to slow his pace of preaching. It was relentless. Listeners were enthralled by both his words and his delivery. His ability to capture people's imaginations, drawing vivid pictures of biblical events, was as strong as ever.

A shipbuilder refused several times to go hear Whitefield speak. Finally, he gave in and went. After the sermon, his friend asked him what he thought of Whitefield's preaching.

"Think," said the shipbuilder, "I never heard such a man in my life." He went on to compare the amount of shipbuilding work he could do in his mind during a normal sermon with the amount he could get done while listening to George Whitefield. "I tell you, sir," he said, "every Sunday, when I go to church, I can build a ship from stem to stern, under the sermon; but, were it to save my soul, under Mr. Whitefield, I could not lay a single plank."

On July 31 George Whitefield sailed from New York to Newport, Rhode Island. He landed on August 3, and with the exception of six days, Whitefield preached every day until he died. On the days when he didn't preach, he was violently ill with diarrhea and other ailments. He traveled throughout northern New England.

The crowds Whitefield faced in New England were different than they had been during earlier trips to the colonies. On the one hand, they seemed more open to his message. But they were also angry over how they were being treated by England. The Boston Massacre, as it came to be called, had taken place that March, and the trial of the British soldiers involved in the incident was scheduled for October.

Whitefield was well aware of the political tensions surrounding him. In a letter to a friend dated September 23, he wrote, "Poor New England is much to be pitied; Boston people most of all. How falsely misrepresented!" Later in the same letter he added, "I am so poorly, and so engaged when able to preach, that this must apologize for not writing to more friends. It is quite impracticable."

It seems Whitefield had determined to use his limited strength to recover from bouts of serious illness, to travel, and to preach—nothing more. On Saturday morning, September 29, he set out from Portsmouth, Massachusetts, to Boston. When he stopped at the village of Exeter, some fifteen miles from Portsmouth, people begged him to give a sermon. A friend observed, "Sir, you are more fit to go to bed than to preach."

Whitefield didn't argue with his friend's assessment, but he agreed to preach anyway. He stood on top of a large barrel to address the crowd. A person who heard him speak described the experience this way: "Mr. Whitefield rose, and stood erect, and his appearance alone was a powerful sermon. He remained several minutes unable to speak; and then said, 'I will wait for the gracious assistance of God; for He will, I am certain, assist me once more to speak in His name.' He then delivered, perhaps, one of his best sermons. 'I go,' he cried, 'I go to a rest prepared. . . . My body fails, my spirit expands. How willingly would I live forever to preach Christ! But I die to be *with* Him.' "

Whitefield's sermon lasted two hours. In his poor health, it was a wonder that he didn't die while preaching. After he finished speaking, his friend, the Reverend Jonathan Parsons, met him. The two dined together and then started for Newburyport, Massachusetts, where Parsons was the Presbyterian minister. When they arrived, Whitefield was so ill that he couldn't leave the boat without assistance.

After an early supper Whitefield was more than ready to retire for the night. "I am tired," he said, "and must go to bed." But a crowd had gathered outside the house. As he headed up the stairs to his room, people at the door begged him to preach. Whitefield couldn't refuse, so he stood on the landing and preached his last sermon. Many sources report that he stopped speaking only when the candle he held flickered, burned itself out, and died away.

A short while after Whitefield retired for the night, he was followed to his room by Richard Smith. "I. . . found him reading the Bible with Dr. Watts' Psalms lying open before him," Smith reported. Whitefield said his evening prayers, talked with Smith for a short while, and then went to sleep. But at about two in the morning, he woke up and asked Smith for something to drink. Smith observed that Whitefield seemed to be panting for breath. Smith asked Whitefield how he was doing.

"He answered, 'My asthma is returning; I must have

two or three days' rest. Two or three days' riding, without preaching, will set me up again.'" Although the window was already halfway open, Whitefield asked Smith to open it a little more. "I cannot breathe," Whitefield said, "but I hope I shall be better by-and-by. A good pulpit sweat today may give me relief. I shall do better after preaching."

When Smith voiced the wish that the older man not preach so often, Whitefield replied, "I had rather wear out, than rust out." After praying about his ministry, the orphanage, the Tabernacle and Chapel in England, and his friends, Whitefield went back to sleep. About forty-five minutes later he woke again, complaining about his breathing. He asked Richard Smith to warm some gruel for him. The sound of Smith breaking some firewood woke their host, Reverend Parsons.

Parsons rushed to Whitefield's side and asked him how he was. "I am almost suffocated," Whitefield said. "I can scarce breathe. My asthma quite chokes me." He moved to a chair by the open window in hopes that the cool air would ease his discomfort. It didn't.

By then it was five o'clock. Richard Smith hurried to Dr. Sawyer's home for assistance. By the time they returned, Whitefield was coughing up phlegm. Dr. Sawyer felt Whitefield's pulse and said, "He is a dead man." Reverend Parsons couldn't believe it. "You must do something, doctor," he said. "I cannot," the doctor replied. "He is now near his last breath."

The doctor's assessment was correct. At six o'clock Sunday morning, September 30, 1770, George Whitefield breathed his last. He was fifty-five years old.

sixteen

News of George Whitefield's death spread quickly through the colonies. Representatives from Boston arrived at the Presbyterian manse in Newburyport, suggesting that Whitefield should be buried in Boston because of its status among the colonies. Many other New Englanders, however, recalled conversations with the itinerant evangelist in which he said that if he died in the colonies, he wanted to be buried under the pulpit of the Presbyterian church in Newburyport.

The Reverend Jonathan Parsons and other officials from his church arranged to carry out Whitefield's request. They constructed a vault underneath the pulpit and announced that the funeral service would be held the afternoon of Tuesday, October 2.

Six ministers, including the first bishop of the Church of England in Massachusetts, served as pallbearers. The funeral procession was a mile long. About six thousand people crammed into the church building, and thousands more lined the procession route. The service included prayers, singing, and a sermon, punctuated by weeping from both the congregation and the ministers. After the service, crowds continued to arrive in Newburyport, begging to be allowed to see the corpse.

Whitefield's death affected thousands of people in different ways. A young man named Benjamin Randall had heard Whitefield speak in Portsmouth, just two days before the preacher's death. Randall didn't like Whitefield. But when a stranger rode through the streets of Portsmouth announcing Whitefield's death, Randall was stunned. He later wrote, "A voice sounded through my soul, more loud and startling than ever thunder pealed upon my ears, *'Whitefield is dead!'* Whitefield is now in heaven, but I am on the road to hell. He was a man of God, and yet I reviled him. He taught me the way to heaven, but I regarded it not. O that I could hear his voice again!"

Benjamin Randall converted to Christianity and became a Baptist minister. He later founded the Free-Will Baptist denomination.

When word of Whitefield's death reached Georgia, colonists were stunned. The pews of the governor and council at the church in Savannah were draped in black, as were the pulpit, chandeliers, and organ. The leaders approved spending money to bring Whitefield's remains to Georgia to be buried at Bethesda, but the people in Newburyport strongly objected. Eventually, the idea was given up, but forty-five years later, when Georgia formed a new county, it was named Whitefield in memory of the man who had done so much for that area.

Among Whitefield's greatest mourners were American

slaves. While his failure to see slavery as evil is justly criticized today, most eighteenth-century slaves considered
Whitefield a friend. He had spoken in their defense and
insisted upon sharing the gospel with them, caring as much
for their souls as for the souls of the highest member of the
British aristocracy. Whenever he could, he also took steps
to see that their living conditions were improved.

Phillis Wheatley, a seventeen-year-old Boston slave
who had converted to Christianity and taught herself to
write poetry with the assistance of her mistress, created
an elegy for George Whitefield. Intended for the
Countess of Huntingdon (mentioned in the last stanza),
it was widely printed and is remarkable for how completely it describes the various aspects of Whitefield's
impact on the American colonies and his insistence that
slaves who turned to Christ would be "sons, and kings,
and priests to God":

> *Hail, happy saint, on thine immortal throne,*
> *Possest of glory, life, and bliss unknown;*
> *We hear no more the music of thy tongue,*
> *Thy wonted auditories cease to throng.*
> *Thy sermons in unequall'd accents flow'd,*
> *And ev'ry bosom with devotion glow'd;*
> *Thou didst in strains of eloquence refin'd*
> *Inflame the heart, and captivate the mind.*
> *Unhappy we the setting sun deplore,*
> *So glorious once, but ah! It shines no more.*
>
> *Behold the prophet in his tow'ring flight!*
> *He leaves the earth for heav'n's unmeasur'd height,*
> *And worlds unknown receive him from our sight.*

There Whitefield *wings with rapid course his way,*
And sails to Zion *through vast seas of day.*
Thy pray'rs, great saint, and thine incessant cries
Have pierc'd the bosom of thy native skies.
Thou moon hast seen, and all the stars of light,
How he has wrestled with his God by night.
He pray'd that grace in ev'ry heart might dwell,
He long'd to see America *excell;*
He charg'd its youth that ev'ry grace divine
Should with full lustre in their conduct shine;
That Saviour, which his soul did first receive,
The greatest gift that ev'n a God can give,
He freely offer'd to the num'rous throng,
That on his lips with list'ning pleasure hung.

"Take him, ye wretched, for your only good,
"Take him ye starving sinners, for your food;
"Ye thirsty, come to this life-giving stream,
"Ye preachers, take him for your joyful theme;
"Take him my dear Americans, *he said,*
"Be your complaints on his kind bosom laid:
"Take him, ye Africans, *he longs for you,*
*"*Impartial Saviour *is his title due:*
"Wash'd in the fountain of redeeming blood,
"You shall be sons, and kings, and priests to God."

Great Countess, *we* Americans *revere*
Thy name, and mingle in thy grief sincere;
New England *deeply feels, the* Orphans *mourn,*
Their more than father will no more return.
But, though arrested by the hand of death,
Whitefield *no more exerts his lab'ring breath,*

192

Yet let us view him in th' eternal skies,
Let ev'ry heart to this bright vision rise;
While the tomb safe retains its sacred trust,
Till life divine re-animates his dust.[1]

Wheatley wasn't alone in her assessment of Whitefield. Many Americans valued him not only for his commitment to evangelism, but also for his sympathy to their complaints against King George III and the British government.

News of Whitefield's death had reached London on November 5. Newspapers and magazines that had followed his work devoted pages to recounting the facts about his life and discussing the impact of his preaching. Friends and fellow ministers gave eulogies to Whitefield in churches all over Great Britain.

Even in death, George Whitefield had a final lesson for his friends. Before he had left England the previous year, Whitefield had told Robert Keen that if he should die, he wanted John Wesley to preach the funeral sermon. It was a fitting tribute to his single-minded determination to find common ground between his Calvinist Methodists and John Wesley.

In his will he left one more surprise. As was the custom at the time, he had set aside money for the purchase of mourning rings to be worn by his friends. Knowing that the contents of his will would certainly appear in print, he had this to say about his final gift to the Wesleys: "I leave a mourning ring to my honoured and dear friends and disinterested fellow-labourers, the Rev. Messrs. John and Charles Wesley, in token of my indissoluble union with them, in heart and Christian affection, notwithstanding our difference in judgment about some particular points of doctrine. Grace be with all of them, of whatever denomination, that love our Lord Jesus, our common Lord, in sincerity." One last time he took pains to publicly declare both his love and respect for the Wesley brothers, and his desire that his followers not allow doctrinal differences to create animosity toward other believers.

When he died, the only money Whitefield possessed was that which had been bequeathed to him by a few supporters and his wife. In his will the bulk of his estate went to support the orphanage. He left the Countess of Huntingdon in charge of the orphanage and the construction of its college.

The first two units of the college were finished in 1773, but then disaster struck. A fire burned the orphanage to the ground. Before the facility could be rebuilt, the Revolutionary War broke out, ending construction.

After the war, the Georgia legislature let the countess retain title to the property even though she was a British subject. She had the best of intentions, but she did not understand how to run the orphanage. She failed to follow Whitefield's pattern of constantly emphasizing Bethesda's contributions to Georgia's economic and moral well-being, a practice that had secured the support of important political leaders. Nor did she have the celebrity status that Whitefield had enjoyed. Even with her influence in the British aristocracy, she could not raise enough money to rebuild Bethesda.

When she died in 1791, the State of Georgia took control of the property and put its care in the hands of a board of trustees. A fire, followed by a hurricane, destroyed the remaining buildings, and in 1808 the board sold its assets. The ministry Whitefield had spent thirty-three years creating ceased to exist.

The Tabernacle in London continued its work for more than a century after Whitefield's death. In 1869 the building was demolished, and a smaller stone structure was built in its place. The stone Tabernacle continued to be a place of ministry until the 1930s when, because the neighborhood had become a commercial district, services were discontinued.

The Tottenham Court Road Chapel continued to attract large crowds, including several members of the nobility. Near the end of World War II, a German rocket destroyed the structure. It was replaced with a smaller building on the original site.

Though George Whitefield had given up official leadership of the Calvinist Methodist societies, those groups maintained close relationships with him up to the time of his death. Many of them continued as active partners with the Church of England in promoting evangelism and discipleship.

When he died, George Whitefield left behind no distinctive theology, no college, no denominational structure. His published sermons and journals are relatively few in number. How are we to assess the impact of a man whose work for God is often obscured by the more familiar accomplishments of John Wesley, Charles Wesley, and Jonathan Edwards? John Wesley himself has given us a place to begin.

In the funeral sermon that he gave for George Whitefield on November 18, 1770, Wesley recounted his friend's life, accomplishments, and beliefs. Among his concluding comments were these words: "Have we read or heard of any person since the apostles, who testified the gospel of the grace of God, through so widely extended a space, through so large a part of the habitable world? Have we read or heard of any person, who called so many thousands, so many myriads of sinners to repentance?"

Perhaps the most important thing to remember about George Whitefield is the expanse of his ministry. Between 1736 and 1770 he peached more than eighteen thousand sermons to audiences both large and small. It is probable that as many as eighty percent of those living in America during that time actually heard Whitefield speak at least once. In all, his audiences numbered in the millions, and millions more were exposed to his words through newspapers, magazines, and printed versions of his sermons, journals, and letters.

Not until the twentieth century, with motion pictures, radio, television, and the Internet, has one person been able to reach so many people across such great distances. Even in our age of satellite communications, it is very difficult for one individual to personally communicate with a majority of any nation's population. But George Whitefield's legacy is not simply a matter of the many individuals who heard or read his words.

As he pursued his evangelistic calling on both sides of the Atlantic, Whitefield created a new type of Christian organization that continues to transform the Church. He developed a ministry that was not officially tied to any denomination and was financially supported by a variety of local churches and individual Christians. The resulting independent base gave him the freedom to pursue the work God had given him, even when denominational leaders tried to ridicule or silence him.

This pattern is still followed by parachurch organizations with all kinds of specialized ministries, such as independent mission agencies, youth and college ministries, and social service organizations. The Salvation Army, Wycliffe Bible Translators, World Vision, Habitat for Humanity, InterVarsity Christian Fellowship, and Young Life are only a few of the thousands of groups that have used the organizational model George Whitefield pioneered.

Whitefield was the first evangelist to exploit the popular media. He used newspapers, religious magazines, pamphlets, posters, and ordinary correspondence to draw huge crowds to his meetings. It did not seem to matter whether the publicity he received was positive or negative, Whitefield almost always found a way to turn it to his advantage and to the advantage of the gospel.

Weeks before he arrived in a town, Whitefield and his supporters would send letters to pastors and other people in the area, letting them know about the upcoming meetings. These supporters, in turn, would contact friends, neighbors, and local newspapers. Some would even hold readings of the letters Whitefield had sent, which often described the work of God in other places. Occasionally a group would meet for several weeks before his appearance and listen to readings from his journals or printed sermons. Whitefield also placed advertisements in newspapers to reach people who otherwise might never hear about him. All this activity was designed to stir up interest during the days leading up to the meetings.

Once he arrived, he spoke wherever he could gather an audience. He seemed just as content to preach in fields, other open areas, or large buildings as he was to speak in traditional churches.

Nineteenth-century evangelist Charles Finney is known today as the Father of Modern Revivalism. Yet Finney himself often identified Whitefield as the innovator whose techniques formed the foundation for his own "new measures."

Whitefield clearly understood the power of newspapers and magazines. His creative use of the eighteenth century's most advanced communications technology set an example that evangelists and other Christian workers have followed ever since. In the early twentieth century, Billy Sunday's messages were transmitted to millions via radio. During the last half of the twentieth century, Billy Graham and those associated with him used television and worldwide satellite communications to reach hundreds of millions at one time. Both evangelists were following in Whitefield's footsteps when they made use of tents, athletic stadiums, and other large venues for their meetings.

As part of his promotional strategy, Whitefield kept records of the size of the crowds who came to hear him and of the number of people responding to his messages. Inspirational stories of what it was like to be involved in these meetings and accounts of actual conversions were circulated by letter among Whitefield's supporters. Both the statistical data and the personal details were later used in publicity campaigns to support future meetings.

By 1950 Billy Graham was keeping records at his evangelistic services for the same reason. He even filmed some of those services from their earliest planning stages through to followup meetings with new believers so that people in other cities could see what a Billy Graham Crusade might be like if it were held in their community.

George Whitefield's greatest personal strength was his dramatic speaking style. He revolutionized preaching in the English-speaking world. Seventy years later John Campbell (a pastor at the London Tabernacle) stated, "The bulk of the best gospel preachers of [Whitefield's] day. . .presented their instruction in a form so scholastic. . . as to require extraordinary intelligence to follow them. . . . But after the star of Whitefield set in, this metaphysical form of instruction gradually disappeared from the British pulpit."

Whitefield had the ability to mesmerize his audiences. In a day when most preachers had adopted the style of a bad academic lecturer, Whitefield's messages were like nothing most people had ever heard. Where most preachers used a complex vocabulary that only a few in their audiences could follow, Whitefield chose simple and direct words that even a child could follow. Where most ministers crafted their sermons to communicate theological ideas, Whitefield focused his attention on the stories and characters of the Old and New Testaments.

He did not simply read these stories; he made them come to life. When he told of Abraham's willingness to sacrifice Isaac, Whitefield's listeners stood with the patriarch on the knife edge between faith and despair. They could sense the son's mounting confusion and fear. They all but collapsed with relief (along with Whitefield) when the ram was found in the thicket. And when George Whitefield spoke of the crucifixion, they could feel the thorns and the nails; they could see the blood.

Whitefield also discussed theological ideas in his sermons, but his approach to these topics linked them to experiences in his own life. His audiences did not simply hear about his conversion experience at Oxford, they lived through it with him.

Whitefield used his whole body to create a dramatic presentation that was more impassioned than the best that the theater of his day had to offer. He often wept during his sermons, and it was never clear whether this was simply a dramatic technique or if he were overcome by the emotion of the moment. Whichever was the case, it is certain that much of the impact Whitefield had on his audiences grew out of the great emotional range he was able to portray.

When John Newton (the former slave ship captain who wrote "Amazing Grace") preached a sermon in tribute to George Whitefield on November 11, 1770, he summed up that impact with these words: "I have had some opportunities of looking over the history of the Church in past ages, and I am not backward to say, that I have not read or heard of any person, since the days of the apostles, of whom it may more emphatically be said, 'He was a burning and shining light,' than of the late Mr. Whitefield. The Lord gave him a manner of preaching, which was peculiarly his own. He copied from none, and I never met any one who could imitate him with success. . . . Other ministers, perhaps, could preach the gospel as clearly, and in general say the same things; but, I believe, no man living could say them in his way. . . . He introduced a way of close and lively application to the conscience for which I believe many of the most admired and eminent preachers now living will not be ashamed, or unwilling to acknowledge themselves his debtors."

The new birth was the central reality of George Whitefield's spiritual life, and practical holiness was his lifelong goal. These things were more important to him than the acceptance of a specific theology, the practice of a particular style of worship, the adoption of one form of church government over another, or loyalty to a single denomination. Though he remained loyal to the Church of England and to Calvinism all his life, his passion was the salvation of the individual.

It did not matter if that individual was rich or poor, male or female, black or white. For George Whitefield, God's offer of salvation in Jesus Christ was so important that all other distinctions had to be set aside. By popularizing the view that everyone had access to God on an equal basis and could experience an unlimited spiritual transformation by entering into the new birth and pursuing practical holiness, Whitefield contributed to an era of revolutionary change that continues to this day.

The idea that everyone has equal value and potential in the sight of God is the philosophical basis for all modern democratic systems of government. It has been one of the driving forces behind a whole series of democratic revolutions that began during Whitefield's life. Though the forces that created the American Revolution shortly after George Whitefield's death are too complex to be explained by a single idea, there is no doubt that Whitefield's individualistic Christianity made an important contribution to American independence.

This same idea of equal human value and potential before God has shaped a vast number of reform movements since Whitefield's day and remains a central assumption in any discussion of human rights.

George Whitefield was one of the first Christian leaders in the post-Reformation world to demonstrate that a life of religious commitment and intensity could reform a society rather than tear it apart.

The people who lived in Great Britain in the middle of the eighteenth century were part of a culture that had only recently escaped from more than two hundred years of religious warfare. A more peaceful atmosphere had been established, but most people still viewed religious "enthusiasm" with suspicion, if not outright fear.

Whitefield's early work, with its emotional appeals and tendency to seek out conflict, concerned them. However, when George Whitefield began to seek reconciliation with John and Charles Wesley and to admit his own mistakes, many people in Great Britain and the American colonies realized they were witnessing a new kind of zeal at work. By the end of his life, Whitefield's example of constructive spiritual passion had made its mark. He would be remembered as both zealous and gentle.

In 1898 no less a person than Charles Spurgeon wrote: "There is no end to the interest which attaches to such a man as George Whitefield. Often as I have read his life, I am conscious of distinct quickening whenever I turn to it. *He lived.* Other men seem to be only half alive; but Whitefield was all life, fire, wing, force. My own model, if I may have such a thing in due subordination to my Lord, is George Whitefield; but with unequal footsteps must I follow in his glorious track."

Whether people agreed with Whitefield or not, by the time he died, the vast majority of them respected him and trusted him. His old friend Benjamin Franklin remained a religious skeptic, but after Whitefield's death he wrote the following tribute in a letter to the Georgia Assembly: "I knew him intimately upwards of thirty years. His Integrity, Disinterestedness, and indefatigable Zeal in prosecuting every good Work, I have never seen equalled, and I shall never see exceeded."[2]

Following in the footsteps of the Puritans and the Quakers, George Whitefield was one of the earliest advocates of treating slaves more humanely. He was the first well-known religious leader of modern times to address their spiritual needs in a serious and consistent way. He went out of his way to make sure that slaves were exposed to the gospel message. By doing this, Whitefield helped lay the foundation for the African-American church. Even though he never opposed slavery directly, his insistence that Jesus had come to redeem blacks as well as whites contributed to the growth of the anti-slavery movement.

During his lifetime, George Whitefield was an immensely influential person. Two words sum up the elements that contributed to that influence: passion and integrity. Of these two, integrity was the most important.

Though vast sums of money passed through his hands, he refused the opportunity to become rich. Though many scandalous stories and jokes were told about Whitefield, there is not the slightest hint of any sexual misconduct by him. Though he clearly enjoyed being famous, he also feared it. Throughout his life he purposely removed himself from positions of power in the church and refused to seek such positions in the secular world. He was, at his core, a man of great integrity because he allowed himself to be transformed by the same new birth he recommended so many times to others.

Notes

Diligent effort has been made to secure permission to use copyrighted material. If any permissions or acknowledgements have been inadvertently omitted, or if such permissions were not received by the time of publication, the publisher would sincerely appreciate receiving complete information so that correct credit can be given in future editions.

Introduction
1. Harry S. Stout, *The Divine Dramatist: George Whitefield and the Rise of Modern Evangelicalism* (Grand Rapids, Mich.: Eerdmans, 1996), 93–94.

Chapter 1
1. Stout, *The Divine Dramatist*, 3.
2. Ibid., 7.
3. Arnold A. Dallimore, *George Whitefield: The Life and Times of the Great Evangelist of the Eighteenth-Century Revival,* vol. 1 (Westchester, Ill.: Cornerstone Books, 1970), 55.

Chapter 2
1. Stout, *The Divine Dramatist,* 18.
2. Ibid., 20–21.

Chapter 4
1. Stout, *The Divine Dramatist,* 73–74.
2. Ibid., 76.
3. Ibid., 78.
4. Ibid., 80.

Chapter 5
1. Stout, *The Divine Dramatist,* 103.
2. Ibid., 110.

Chapter 9
1. Luke Tyerman, *The Life of The Reverend George Whitefield,* vol. 2 (London: Hodder & Stoughton, 1877) reprinted by Need of the Times Publishers, Azle, Tex., 1995, p. 277.

Chapter 12
1. Stout, *The Divine Dramatist,* 239.

Chapter 16
1. Phillis Wheatley, "On the Death of the Rev. Mr. George Whitefield." Available on the internet at darkwing.uoregon.edu/~rbear/wheatley.html.
2. Stout, *The Divine Dramatist,* 286–87.

Bibliography

Dallimore, Arnold A. *George Whitefield: The Life and Times of the Great Evangelist of the Eighteenth-Century Revival.* 2 vols. Westchester, Ill.: Cornerstone Books, 1980.

Dallimore, Arnold A. *George Whitefield: God's Anointed Servant in the Great Revival of the Eighteenth Century.* Wheaton, Ill.: Crossway Books, 1990.

Franklin, Benjamin. *The Autobiography of Benjamin Franklin.* New Haven, Conn.: Yale Univ. Press, 1964.

George Whitefield. *Christian History,* vol. XII, no. 2, issue 38 (1993).

Lambert, Frank. *"Pedlar in Divinity": George Whitefield and the Transatlantic Revivals.* Princeton, N.J.: Princeton Univ. Press, 1994.

Stout, Harry S. *The Divine Dramatist: George Whitefield and the Rise of Modern Evangelicalism.* Grand Rapids, Mich.: Eerdmans, 1996.

Tyerman, Luke. *The Life of The Reverend George Whitefield.* 2 vols. 1877. Reprint, Azle, Tex.: Need of the Times, 1995.

Whitefield, George. *George Whitefield's Journals.* 1738–41, 1747, 1756. Reprint, Carlisle, Penn.: The Banner of Truth Trust, 1960.

HEROES OF THE FAITH